This is the first major anthology of poems about dogs and is a companion to the successful volume *The Poetry of Horses* also collected by Olwen Way.

The poems cover the whole spectrum from the classical Greek to contemporary poets published here for the first time. The familiar and the accessible are included as well as the classical and lesser-known. The poems and extracts contained in this volume explore the life of the dog from birth to death, look at different breeds and activities, and in particular reflect dog's relationship with man.

With delightful illustrations drawn especially for the poems by talented animal artist, Maggie Raynor, this book will be picked up again and again, to renew old acquaintances, to make new friends, and to satisfy all moods. Through its pages the poetry lover will come to know dogs and the dog lover will come to know poetry.

THE
POETRY
OF
DOGS

A COLLECTION BY
Olwen Way

ILLUSTRATED BY
Maggie Raynor

J. A. Allen
London

British Library Cataloguing-in-Publication Data
A catalogue record for this book is available from the British Library

ISBN 0.85131.788X

Published in Great Britain in 2000 by J. A. Allen
An imprint of Robert Hale Ltd
Clerkenwell House, 45–47 Clerkenwell Green, London, ECIR OHT

Designed by Nancy Lawrence
Edited by Elizabeth O'Beirne-Ranelagh

Printed in Hong Kong by Dah Hua Printing Press Co. Ltd.

CONTENTS

ACKNOWLEDGEMENTS

Once again I would like to thank my son, Gregory Way, for the use of his library.

I would also like to thank Elizabeth O'Beirne-Ranelagh, Nancy Lawrence and Maggie Raynor at J. A. Allen, and their team who helped to put this book together.

Olwen Way

DEDICATION

To the memory of Ted –
an English Pointer.

INTRODUCTION

In this collection of poems, I have tried to show the bond between dogs and humans. Many of the poems are about real relationships, very often concerned with the pain of loss and reality of grieving over a beloved dog, but there are also poems exploring the mythical, mysterious and touching.

Since man and dog first befriended each other in the mists of time, the dog has been a symbol in many cultures. I have tried to include a mixed kennel – pedigree dogs, famous dogs, dogs in relation to children, working dogs – and a number of eulogies and epitaphs. I hope that some readers will find a mention of their own favourite breed or of characters like dogs they love or have loved, and that others will gain from reading again or for the first time stories of dogs like Argos and Gelert, who stand as symbols for so many brave and faithful dogs who never had poems made for them.

Some of the greatest poets in the English language are included, both from past centuries and from today, as well as a number of poets who are published here for the first time, or who have produced a poem especially for this anthology. Like its sister volume, *The Poetry of Horses*, this anthology is designed both to be dipped into and to be read from beginning to end in a spirit of adventure, each poem linked by thread or theme to the following one. Thus we start with Kipling's heartfelt poem, 'The power of the dog', which gives us the theme of the book overall and leads into a set of poems exploring the closeness between dog and owner, and the friendship and companionship which results from the bond. Elizabeth Barrett Browning's famous pet, Flush, shows how the dog comforts in times of sorrow and difficulty, and her poem is the first of a group where the dog acts as catalyst in the relationship between man and woman. Oliver Goldsmith's well-known poem, 'On the death of a mad dog', is the first of a series on the wild side of the dog and his wolf ancestors, which is then compared with the loyalty of the domestic dog. A large section follows describing many different breeds of dog, from spaniels and pointers to Newfoundlands and greyhounds. The need to destroy an old dog or an unwanted dog is expressed by Norman MacCaig and Thomas Hardy, and themes of betrayal and rescue highlight the inexhaustible wish of the dog to please its owner. The fun and humorous side of the dog and its relationship with children is balanced by the sadness and blackness of its death, and the descriptions of well-loved dogs extend into a longer section on doggy characters of every sort, culminating in William Cowper's two beautiful and most pleasing poems about his spaniel Beau.

Pope's amusing couplet, 'Kew', prefaces a section where it is the dog who is left to mourn its owner, and an examination of the ways in which a dog supports its owner through work, bravery and loyalty leads to a number of poems which express in many different ways the desire of the owner to find his or her dog again after death. Religious themes explore man's inhumanity to man and beast, and Spike Milligan's 'The dog lovers' shows the unwitting cruelty which can occur. A series of linking poems brings us to a section on hounds and hunting dogs, with poets from the sixteenth century to the modern day describing the dog's love of the chase, whether organised or for its own pleasure. T. S. Eliot and Roger McGough are among the poets who have written humorous or whimsical celebrations of the dog, and Ted Hughes' 'Roger the dog' changes the mood briefly to sleeping dogs, or those that wait patiently for the best moment of their day – the walk!

The energy of the dog at exercise is wonderfully captured by a number of authors, and this energy is also seen in puppies, who 'Buffet each other with their duffer paws' in Vita Sackville-West's 'The land'. But youth is eventually followed by old age, possibly abandonment, and death. The understanding of the bond between owner and dog is most touchingly described in Sir Henry Newbolt's poem, 'Fidele's grassy tomb', and a number of poems express the bond between the working dog and its master. But once again it is the depth of feeling at the loss of a true friend which is the theme of the last few poems in the collection, and Kipling brings us full circle with 'Four-feet', a reminder that as hard as we try, we cannot altogether lose the memory of that special relationship with a special dog.

RUDYARD KIPLING
The Power of the Dog

There is sorrow enough in the natural way
From men and women to fill our day;
And when we are certain of sorrow in store,
Why do we always arrange for more?
Brothers and Sisters, I bid you beware
Of giving your heart to a dog to tear.

Buy a pup and your money will buy
Love unflinching that cannot lie –
Perfect passion and worship fed
By a kick in the ribs or a pat on the head.
Nevertheless it is hardly fair
To risk your heart for a dog to tear.

When the fourteen years which Nature permits
Are closing in asthma, or tumour, or fits,
And the vet's unspoken prescription runs
To lethal chambers or loaded guns,
Then you will find – it's your own affair –
But . . . you've given your heart to a dog to tear.

When the body that lived at your single will,
With its whimper of welcome, is stilled (how still!)
When the spirit that answered your every mood
Is gone – wherever it goes – for good,
You will discover how much you care,
And will give your heart to a dog to tear.

We've sorrow enough in the natural way,
When it comes to burying Christian clay.
Our loves are not given, but only lent,
At compound interest of cent per cent.
Though it is not always the case, I believe,
That the longer we've kept 'em, the more do we
    grieve:
For, when debts are payable, right or wrong,
A short-time loan is as bad as a long –
So why in – Heaven (before we are there)
Should we give our hearts to a dog to tear?

[2]

SIR JOHN SQUIRE
A Dog's Death

The loose earth falls in the grave like a peaceful
    regular breathing;
Too like, for I was deceived a moment by the sound:
It has covered the heap of bracken that the gardener
    laid above him;
Quiet the spade swings: there we have now his
    mound.

A patch of fresh earth on the floor of the wood's
    renewing chamber:
All around is grass and moss and the hyacinth's dark
    green sprouts:
And oaks are above that were old when his fiftieth
    sire was a puppy:
And far away in the garden I hear the children's
    shouts.

Their joy is remote as a dream. It is strange how we
    buy our sorrow
For the touch of perishing things, idly, with open eyes;
How we give our hearts to brutes that will die in a
    few seasons,
Nor trouble what we do when we do it; nor would
    have it otherwise.

eℛ

[3]

SIEGFRIED SASSOON
Man and Dog

eℛ

Who's this – alone with stone and sky?
It's only my old dog and I –
It's only him; it's only me;
Alone with stone and grass and tree.

What share we most – we two together?
Smells, and awareness of the weather.
What is it makes us more than dust?
My trust in him; in me his trust.

Here's anyhow one decent thing
That life to man and dog can bring;
One decent thing, remultiplied
Till earth's last dog and man have died.

[4]

ELEANOR FARJEON
Inside

A bellyfull and the fire,
And him in his old suit,
And me with my heart's desire,
My head across his foot.

And I doze. And he reads.
And the clock ticks slow.
And, though he never heeds,
He knows, and I know.

Presently, without look,
His hand will feel to tug
My ear, his eyes on book,
Mine upon the rug.

[5]

ADRIAN MITCHELL
To my Dog
❧

This gentle beast
This golden beast
laid her long chin
along my wrist

and my wrist
is branded
with her love
and trust

and the salt of my cheek
is hers to lick
so long as I
or she shall last

❧

[6]

CECIL FLOERSHEIM
To my Dog
❧

Comrade, whose muzzle gray-besprent
Nods lower now from head earth-bent;
Whose halting gait makes evident
    That time goes faster;

Who follow where you used to lead;
And, for the voice you seldom heed,
Pursue a weary shade indeed,
      To please your master.

In this enfeebled age and lone,
That lags, to wise indifference grown,
Serene would I foresee my own
      In its declining;

Still envious to outsleep the dew,
Yet, prompted by the voice it knew,
Content a shadow to pursue
      Without repining.

Yes, brown eyes tremulously bright,
No loss have you, though dimmed your sight,
And gone the force that took delight
      In its own fleetness;

For joy is yours by habit willed,
And trust that hears though ear be stilled,
And faith, and love that is fulfilled
      With incompleteness.

RUTH SKILLING
Full Circle

When John was ten they gave the boy
(A farmer's son) no passing toy,
But his own sheep-dog, eight weeks old.
They'd play round barn and rick and fold
Till running, John would turn to find
His puppy sitting far behind.
With puzzled look and whimpers he
Would plead, 'O master, wait for me!'

The years sped on. Through wind and weather
The boy and dog grew up together.
On hill and dale, through heath and fern,
Nor did John need to slow and turn.
When rounding sheep the dog roamed wide
Outstripping far his master's stride;
He'd work the flock, his joy – his pride –
With whistles only as a guide.

And twelve years on the dog was still
A close companion on the hill,
But in the truck he'd often stay
And guard the gear. Now growing grey
In cheek and muzzle, when again
They strolled together down the lane,
He'd pant and pause, and sightless he
Would plead, 'O master, wait for me!'

JOHN GALSWORTHY
To my Dog

My dear, when I leave you
I always drop a bit of me –
A holy glove or sainted shoe –
Your wistful corse I leave it to,
For all your soul has followed me
How could I have the stony head
So to abandon you!

My dear when you leave me,
You drop no glove, no sainted shoe;
And yet you know what humans be –
Mere blocks of dull monstrosity –
My spirit cannot follow you
When you're away, with all its heart
As yours can follow me.

My dear, since we must leave
(One sorry day) I you, you me;
I'll learn your wistful way to grieve;
Then through the ages we'll retrieve
Each other's scent and company;
And longing shall not pull my heart –
As now you my sleeve!

OGDEN NASH
The Dog

∽

The truth I do not stretch or shove
When I state the dog is full of love.
I've also proved by actual test
A wet dog is the lovingest.

∽

[10]

NATHANIEL GIMSON
Sorrel

∽

Sorrel, to me, is loving,
A loving, golden, bouncy friend
As she bounds along,
Her thick coat waving in the breeze
She means the world to me!

Her ears prick as the pheasants fall
Raring to go
Raring to retrieve the lying birds
Now she jumps, now she ducks
All for the praise of the humans

But now she lies, dreaming
Of the day's work
Waiting for another day
Waiting for it to happen again.

[11]

OLWEN WAY

A Shakespearian Sonnet for Ted

My dog comes racing to me, ears alert,
Jaws open in a moment of pure joy,
Long legs comb August broom and skirt
The fringe of grasses spread as its alloy.
At one with life, exuberant he lives
A purity of joy I cannot share.

The lack of complication that he gives
Each moment, shot through with transcendent
    power –
Maybe it's true that we acknowledge death
And so are out of kilter, out of joint,
Eleven now, he bounds and rests, takes breath
Nature takes hold, to let my pointer point.
Why does a sudden shaft of prescient pain
Force me to see an empty field again?

J. N. A.

Elegy on a Retriever Dog

Which, after accompanying its master through the
Affghan Campaign with Sir W. Knott, in 1842, died
in Guzerat the following year.

Rest here in peace, my Carlos, where flickering
  branches wave,
And dews their daily tribute shed upon thy grassy
  grave.
Far may thy master wander, and many a region
  view,
Or e'er he find a friend than thee more gentle and
  more true.

Fond memory shall recall thee; affection shall retrace
Thy sparkling eye, thy winning way, thy form of
     matchless grace,
Thy beauteous limbs, thy bounding step, that flew
     o'er hill and lea:
Where, where shall I behold again another dog like
     thee?

Thou wert no home-bred idler, in pampered luxury
     nursed;
Thy course was noble as thy form, and marked thee
     with the first.
Full many a travelled sage would joy to be where thou
     hast been,
And many a warrior's heart would leap to see what
     thou hast seen.

Realms rich in classic story, far distant, hast thou
     trod,
Where Philip's son his conquests won, and Grecian
     cohorts strode;
Where Bactrian kings their sceptres swayed, and from
     whose peaks of snow
Duranee chiefs like whirlwinds lashed and swept the
     plains below.

All those broad lands and fertile fields thy foot hath
     wandered o'er,
Through which the five great rivers their circling
     eddies pour,
And where those rivers join in one, and Indus, broad
     and free,
His mighty tribute rolls along to swell the Arabian sea.

Full oft I've smiled to see thee in that mimic ocean's
    wave,
With joyous cry leap from on high, thy wavy locks to
    lave, –
And bravely o'er the foaming flood thy face of joy
    upbore,
While shouted all admiring praise and welcomed thee
    to shore.

Not all thy course was playful: nine times in stricken
    field
War's thunders hast thou heard, and seen the Moslem
    Crescent yield;
In Kandahar and Ghuznee seen, on Cabul's turrets
    high,
The waving flag of Britain's hosts that told of victory!

Now all these scenes are ended; thy joys and pains are
    o'er; –
My guard by night, my friend by day, I greet thee now
    no more.
Ere twice ten moons had o'er thee passed, and
    scarcely yet in bloom,
Disease had struck with withering blast, and swept
    thee to the tomb.

Then rest thee here, my Carlos. Heaven grant thy
    master prove
No less than thee in gratitude, fidelity, and love!
When thy example I recall, superior though I be,
The man may by the brute be taught, and I may learn
    from thee.

DEREK NEVILLE

The Little Dog from Nowhere

Old Charlie had no friend
And he lived the other end
Of Main Street in a tumbledown old shed.

It was very nearly dark
When he heard a sudden bark
From a little dog from nowhere by his bed.

He was lost and he was tired.
He was hungry, he was scared,
Just a little dog from nowhere in the dark.

He had seen a gleam of light,
Like an opening in the night,
From a tumbledown old shed outside the park.

Old Charlie, all alone,
Gave the little dog a bone;
Took him in and let him lie upon a sack.

As he came in from the cold,
All the night was sudden gold,
For the little dog from nowhere in the shack.

Now Charlie swindled folks galore,
With every other breath, he swore.
He'd con each man or woman he could find.

He cheated all the way
With petty crimes each day.
They said he'd take a shilling from the blind!

And the folks – they used to shun him,
Look right through him, or above him,
Till the little dog from nowhere came around.

Charles was dirty, he was cheap,
He was nothing but a creep.
He had lost all self-respect, so it would seem.

But he was all that mattered
To the little dog that pattered
And followed him as if he were a dream.

With his little head held high,
And his tail towards the sky,
It would follow him as if he were a king.

Every morning they would pass
Through the fragrant meadow-grass,
And the folks who saw forgave him everything.

And I guess that here's a story
With a wealth of hidden glory.
Folk came to know the two of them as one.

And in the end what counted
Was a real respect that mounted
– That the little dog from nowhere had begun.

When they saw him on the street,
All the folks would turn and greet him.
'Mornin' Charlie!' 'Howya, Charlie?' they would cry.

For the man without a friend
– He had found one in the end
– In a little dog from nowhere walking high.

[14]

J. T. TROWBRIDGE
The Vagrant and His Dog

We are two travellers, Roger and I.
   Roger's my dog. Come here, you scamp!
Jump for the gentleman, – mind your eye!
   Over the table, look out for the lamp!

The rogue is growing a little old;
    Five years we've tramped through wind and
        weather,
And slept out-doors when nights were cold,
    And ate and drank – and starved – together.

We've learned what comfort is, I tell you!
    A bed on the floor, a bit of rosin,
A fire to thaw our thumbs (poor fellow!
    The paw he holds up there's been frozen),
Plenty of catgut for my fiddle,
    (This out-door business is bad for strings,)
Then a few nice buckwheats hot from the
        griddle,
    And Roger and I set up for kings!

No, thank ye, sir, – I never drink;
    Roger and I are exceedingly moral, –
Aren't we, Roger? – See him wink!
    Well, something hot, then, we won't quarrel.
He's thirsty too, – see him nod his head?
    What a pity, sir, that dogs can't talk!
He understands every word that's said, –
    And he knows good milk from water and chalk.

The truth is, sir, now I reflect,
    I've been so sadly given to grog,
I wonder I've not lost the respect
    (Here's to you, sir!) even of my dog.
But he sticks by me through thick and thin;
    And this old coat, with its empty pockets,
And rags that smell of tobacco and gin,
    He'll follow while he has eyes in his sockets.

There isn't another creature living
    Would do it, and prove, through every disaster,
So fond, so faithful, and so forgiving,
    To such a miserable thankless master!
No, sir! – see him wag his tail and grin!
    By George! it makes my old eyes water!
That is, there's something in this gin
    That chokes a fellow. But no matter!

We'll have some music, if you're willing,
    And Roger (hem! what a plague a cough is, sir!)
Shall march a little. – Start, you villain!
    Stand straight! 'Bout face! Salute your officer!

Put up that paw! Dress! Take your rifle!
   (Some dogs have arms, you see!) Now hold your
Cap while the gentlemen give a trifle,
   To aid a poor old patriotic soldier!

March! Halt! Now show how the rebel shakes,
   When he stands up to hear his sentence;
Now tell us how many drams it takes
   To honour a jolly new acquaintance.
Five yelps, – that's five; he's mighty knowing!
   The night's before us, fill the glasses! _
Quick sir! I'm ill, – my brain is going! –
   Some brandy, – thank you, – there! – it passes!

. . .

Another glass, and strong to deaden
   This pain; then Roger and I will start.
I wonder has he such a lumpish, leaden,
   Aching thing, in place of a heart?
He is sad sometimes, and would weep if he could,
   No doubt remembering things that were, –
A virtuous kennel, with plenty of food,
   And himself a sober, respectable cur.

I'm better now; that glass was warming. –
   You rascal! limber your lazy feet!
We must be fiddling and performing
   For supper and bed, or starve in the street. –
Not a very gay life to lead, you think?
   But soon we shall go where lodgings are free,
And the sleepers need neither victuals nor drink;
   The sooner the better for Roger and me!

WILLIAM WORDSWORTH
FROM
The Prelude

Among the favourites whom it pleased me well
To see again was one by ancient right
Our intimate, a rough terrier of the hills;
By birth and call of nature preordained
To hunt the badger and unearth the fox
Among the impervious crags, but having been
From youth our own adopted he had passed
Into a gentler service. And when first

The boyish spirit flagged, and day by day
Along my veins I kindled with the stir,
The fermentation and the vernal heat
Of poesy, affecting private shades
Like a sick lover, then this dog was used
To watch me, an attendant and a friend,
Obsequious to my steps early and late,
Though often of such dilatory walk
Tired, and uneasy of the halts I made.
A hundred times when roving high and low,
I have been harassed with the toil of verse,
Much pains and little progress, and at once
Some lovely image in the song rose up
Full-formed, like Venus rising from the sea;
Then have I darted forward to let loose
My hand upon his back with stormy joy,
Caressing him again and yet again.
And when at evening on the public way
I sauntered like a river murmuring
And talking to itself when all things else
Are still, the creature trotted on before;
Such was his custom; But whene'er he met
A passenger approaching, he would turn
To give me timely notice.

EDWARD THOMAS
Man and Dog

''Twill take some getting.' 'Sir, I think 'twill so.'
The old man stared up at the mistletoe
That hung too high in the poplar's crest for plunder
Of any climber, though not for kissing under:
Then he went on against the north-east wind –
Straight but lame, leaning on a staff new-skinned,
Carrying a brolly, flag-basket, and old coat, –
Towards Alton, ten miles off. And he had not
Done less from Chilgrove where he pulled up docks.
'Twere best, if he had had 'a money-box,'
To have waited there till the sheep cleared a field
For what a half-week's flint-picking would yield.
His mind was running on the work he had done
Since he left Christchurch in the New Forest, one
Spring in the 'seventies, – navvying on dock and line
From Southampton to Newcastle-on-Tyne, –
In 'seventy-four a year of soldiering
With the Berkshires, – hoeing and harvesting
In half the shires where corn and couch will grow.
His sons, three sons, were fighting, but the hoe
And reap-hook he liked, or anything to do with trees.
He fell once from a poplar tall as these:
The Flying Man they called him in hospital.
'If I flew now, to another world I'd fall.'
He laughed and whistled to the small brown bitch
With spots of blue that hunted in the ditch.
Her foxy Welsh grandfather must have paired
Beneath him. He kept sheep in Wales and scared

Strangers, I will warrant, with his pearl eye
And trick of shrinking off as he *was* shy,
Then following close in silence for – for what?
'No rabbit, never fear, she ever got,
Yet always hunts. To-day she nearly had one:
She would and she wouldn't. 'Twas like that. The bad
    one!
She's not much use, but still she's company,
Though I'm not. She goes everywhere with me.
So Alton I must reach to-night somehow:
I'll get no shakedown with that bedfellow
From farmers. Many a man sleeps worse to-night
Than I shall.' 'In the trenches.' 'Yes, that's right.
But they'll be out of that – I hope they be –
This weather, marching after the enemy.'
'And so I hope. Good luck.' And there I nodded
'Good-night. You keep straight on.' Stiffly he plodded;
And at his heels the crisp leaves scurried fast,
And the leaf-coloured robin watched. They passed,
The robin till next day, the man for good,
Together in the twilight of the wood.

P. HORRIDGE
The Partners

∾

Devout Miss Talbot, maiden sixty-nine,
Is torn from blameless dreams before she would;
Beside her bedsit bed with yapping whine
The bulge-eyed scrap of poodle, screams for food.
With tiny sigh she rises to the cold
Her white and withered limbs in flannel gown,
And starts this morning new with routine old
As grey light spreads across the waking town.
First, fresh warmed milk in saucer by the fire,
(For gas a shilling) loud the poodle laps,
Then heat the broth prepared the night before
With carefully chopped selected rabbit scraps.
The doggy plate washed clean as it could be
(No soap detergent!) Dried with loving care –
Newspaper on the floor meticulously
In his selected spot – a folded square,
Next test the temperature, cut the large bits fine,
Remove what might be gristle, bone or skin:
Then, harassed by his leaping, yap and whine –
Flustered, put down the plate and he begins.
No time then to do more than swiftly dress –
A puddle by the door for all her haste –
No heed for feeble scoldings at the mess
But tugs her to the park with bouncing zest.
Careful itinerary, skirting suspect spots,
Where dirt, cats, other dogs might chance to be:
Prancing on pretty lead he lightly trots
She shortly steps, sedate with dignity.

Then home and while he sleeps on tidied bed
She breakfasts, brown bread, tea that's stewed
  as brown
Then, greatly daring, prey to guilty dread,
Leaves him – to scurry shopping in the town.
His luncheon bought, again the rigmarole
Of cooking, preparation, serve with fuss;
Visit the vet on the post-prandial stroll
Neat questions on his welfare to discuss.
Finally at evening, home for last repast –
The most elaborate, careful of the day,
Her frugal supper too – one day more passed,
In spectacles she reads: sleep has its way.

All the to-morrows echo this to-day –
Her life round him revolves, his rests on hers:
Thus do they keep old loneliness at bay,
Miss Talbot, and her poodle – and the years!

THOM GUNN
Her Pet

~

I walk the floor, read, watch a cop-show, drink,
Hear buses heave uphill through drizzling fog,
Then turn back to the pictured book to think
Of Valentine Balbiani and her dog:
She is reclining, reading, on her tomb;
But pounced, it tries to intercept her look,
Its front paws on her lap, as in this room
The cat attempts to nose beneath my book.

Her curls tight, breasts held by her bodice high,
Ruff crisp, mouth calm, hands long and delicate,
All in the pause of marble signify
A strength so lavish she can limit it.
She will not let her pet dog catch her eye
For dignity, and for a touch of wit.

Below, from the same tomb, is reproduced
A side-relief, in which she reappears
Without her dog, and everything is loosed –
Her hair down from the secret of her ears,
Her big ears, and her creased face genderless
Craning from sinewy throat. Death is so plain!
Her breasts are low knobs through the unbound
    dress.
In the worked features I can read the pain
She went through to get here, to shake it all,
Thinking at first that her full nimble strength
Hid like a little dog within recall,

Till to think so, she knew, was to pretend
And, hope dismissed, she sought out pain at length
And laboured with it to bring on its end.

[19]
ELIZABETH BARRETT BROWNING
Flush or Faunus

You see this dog. It was but yesterday
I mused forgetful of his presence here
Till thought on thought drew downward tear on tear,
When from the pillow where wet-cheeked I lay,
A head as hairy as Faunus, thrust its way
Right sudden against my face, – two golden-clear

Great eyes astonished mine, – a drooping ear
Did flap on either cheek to dry the spray!
I started first, as some Arcadian,
Amazed by goatly god in twilight grove:
But as the bearded vision closlier ran
My tears off, I knew Flush and rose above
Surprise and sadness, – thanking the true Pan
Who, by low creatures, leads to heights of love.

[20]

ALGERNON CHARLES SWINBURNE
FROM
Tristram of Lyonesse

But that same night in Cornwall oversea
Couched at Queen Iseult's hand, against her knee,
With keen kind eyes that read her whole heart's pain
Fast at wide watch lay Tristram's hound Hodain,
The goodliest and the mightiest born on earth,
That many a forest day of fiery mirth
Had plied his craft before them; and the queen
Cherished him, even for those dim years between,
More than of old in those bright months far flown
When ere a blast of Tristram's horn was blown
Each morning as the woods rekindled, ere
Day gat full empire of the glimmering air,
Delight of dawn would quicken him, and fire
Spring and pant in his breath with bright desire
To be among the dewy ways on quest:

But now perforce at restless-hearted rest
He chafed through days more barren than the sand,
Soothed hardly but soothed only with her hand,
Though fain to fawn thereon and follow, still
With all his heart and all his loving will
Desiring one divided from his sight,
For whose lost sake dawn was as dawn of night
And noon as night's noon in his eyes was dark.

. . .

And Iseult, worn with watch long held on pain,
Turned, and her eye lit on the hound Hodain,
And all her heart went out in tears: and he
Laid his kind head along her bended knee,
Till round his neck her arms went hard, and all
The night past from her as a chain might fall:
But yet the heart within her, half undone,
Wailed, and was loth to let her see the sun.

[21]

ANN SMITH
Sonnet

'Do you think I could replace you with a terrier?'
'I'd like to think you can't, but fear you could.'
Would a dog make me as happy, even merrier?
Could a dog keep me in such a buoyant mood?
A dog would give me love and keep me company,
A dog would snuggle up and keep me warm.

A dog would take my side against an enemy,
And help me with the chores around the farm.
A dog would let me cry on to its shoulder
And look at me with sympathetic eyes,
And wouldn't notice that I'm growing older –
And would give me its devotion till it dies.
 But I'll never love a dog as I've loved you,
 Although in truth a dog may have to do.

[22]

JO SHAPCOTT
Muse

When I kiss you in all the folding places
of your body, you make that noise like a dog
dreaming, dreaming of the long runs he makes
in answer to some jolt to his hormones,
running across landfills, running, running
by tips and shorelines from the scent of too much,
but still going with head up and snout
in the air because he loves it all
and has to get away. I have to kiss deeper
and more slowly – your neck, your inner arm,

the neat creases under your toes, the shadow
behind your knee, the white angles of your groin –
until you fall quiet because only then
can I get the damned words to come into my mouth.

[23]

SIR JOHN HARINGTON
To his Wife, for Striking her Dog

Your little Dog that bark'd as I came by,
I strake by hap so hard, I made him cry,
And straight you put your finger in your eye
And low'ring sate, I ask'd the reason why.
'Love me and love my Dog,' thou didst reply:
'Love, as both should be lov'd.' 'I will,' said I,
And seal'd it with a kisse. Then by and by
Clear'd were the clouds of thy faire frowning skie;
Thus small events great masteries may try.
For I by this do at their meaning guesse,
That beat a whelpe afore a lyonesse!

PATRICK CHALMERS
To Nell

∽

Come here young woman; while we wait my chance is
   To speak a word in your betendrilled ear;
Think not to put me off with melting glances,
   Prop of your sex when censure looms a-near,
   With slavish smirk or adulating leer;
I'm not the man, by commonest consent,
     To bow to blandishment.

I know you love me, and I hope you honour;
   I want to be as sure about *obey*;
E'en when temptations fall most thick upon her
   No lady should, I think, break clean away;
   Her youth may trifle with some fancy gay,
But prompt she heeds, be she of good repute,
     Her lord's 'Come in, you brute!'

Be circumspect, my pretty one; be steady,
   Though Fur all feminine endurance tests;
Thus, the drive done, we'll have you here and ready
   Tenderly busy on my right behests,
   The cynosure of gamekeepers and guests;
While e'en Sir John, with laudatory pat,
     Says, 'Topping spaniel, that!'

∽

OGDEN NASH
Love Me but Leave my Dog Alone

Once there was a handsome man named Mr
    Beamington and he was to good causes the most
    generous of donors,
And he was so popular with dogs that he couldn't
    understand why he was so unpopular with their
    owners.
He was bold as an eagle, a cock eagle, yet gentle as a
    dove, a hen-dove,
And the dog didn't live that he couldn't make a friend of.
If you had a brace of ferocious spaniels
Mr Beamington would soon be romping with them
    through your annuals and peranniels.
He fondled schnauzers
With no scathe to his trousers.
At his voice the pit bull eschewed the manners of the
    bull pit,
And assumed those of the pulpit.
He could discuss Confucianism with a Pekinese,
And address the Boston terrier on Beacon Hill in
    purest Beaconese.
Yes, Mr Beamington had a way with dogs, dogs
    simply adored him,
Yet their owners abhorred him,
Because he reckoned without the third law of
    Paracelsus,
Which clearly states that every dog-owner considers
    his dog a one-man dog, and its affection his own
    and nobody elsus.

So the only people who liked him were the owners of
    a Cairn,
Which frequently bit him, thus reassuring them that
    its heart was not hisn but theirn.

                e⁓

[26]

OLIVER GOLDSMITH
On the Death of a Mad Dog
e⁓

Good people all, of every sort,
    Give ear unto my song;
And if you find it wondrous short,
    It cannot hold you long.

In Islington there was a man,
    Of whom the world might say,
That still a godly race he ran
    Whene'er he went to pray.

A kind and gentle heart he had,
    To comfort friends and foes;
The naked every day he clad,
    When he put on his clothes.

And in that town a dog was found,
    As many dogs there be,
Both mongrel, puppy, whelp, and hound,
    And curs of low degree.

This dog and man at first were friends;
    But when a pique began,
The dog, to gain his private ends,
    Went mad and bit the man.

Around from all the neighbouring streets
    The wondering neighbours ran,
And swore the dog had lost his wits,
    To bite so good a man.

The wound it seem'd both sore and sad
    To every Christian eye:
And while they swore the dog was mad,
    They swore the man would die.

But soon a wonder came to light,
    That show'd the rogues they lied,
The man recover'd of the bite,
    The dog it was that died.

GEORGE CRABBE
Fang

There watch'd a cur before the Miser's gate –
A very cur, whom all men seem'd to hate:
Gaunt, savage, shaggy, with an eye that shone
Like a live coal, and he possess'd but one;
His bark was wild and eager, and became
That meagre body and that eye of flame;
His master prized him much, and *Fang* his name
His master fed him largely; but not that,
Nor aught of kindness, made the snarler fat.

Flesh he devour'd, but not a bit would stay;
He bark'd and snarl'd, and growl'd it all away.
His ribs were seen extending like a rack,
And coarse red hair hung roughly o'er his back.
Lamed in one leg, and bruised in wars of yore,
Now his sore body made his temper sore.
Such was the friend of him who could not find
Nor make him one 'mong creatures of his kind.
Brave deeds of Fang his master often told,
The son of Fury, famed in deeds of old,
From Snatch and Rabid sprung; and noted they
In earlier times – each dog will have his day.
The notes of Fang were to his master known,
And dear – they bore some likeness to his own:
For both conveyed to his experienced ear,
'I snarl and bite, because I hate and fear.'
None passed ungreeted by the master's door, –
Fang railed at all, but chiefly at the poor;

And when the nights were stormy, cold and dark,
The act of Fang was a perpetual bark;
But though the master loved the growl of Fang,
There were who vow'd the ugly cur to hang;
Whose angry master, watchful for his friend,
As strongly vow'd his servant to defend.

In one dark night, and such as Fang before
Was ever known its tempests to outroar,
To his protector's wonder now express'd
No angry notes – his anger was at rest.
The wondering master sought the silent yard,
Left Phœbe sleeping and his door unbarr'd;
No more returned to that forsaken bed –
But lo! the morning came and he was dead.

Fang and his master side by side were laid
In grim repose – their debt of nature paid!
The master's hand upon the cur's cold chest
Was now reclined and had before been press'd,
As if he search'd how deep and wide the wound
That laid such spirit in a sleep so sound;
And when he found it was the sleep of death,
A sympathising sorrow stopp'd his breath.
Close to his trusty servant he was found,
As cold his body, and his sleep as sound.

IRENE McLEOD
Lone Dog

I'm a lean dog, a keen dog, a wild dog and lone,
I'm a rough dog, a tough dog, hunting on my own!
I'm a bad dog, a mad dog, teasing silly sheep;
I love to sit and bay the moon and keep fat souls from
sleep.

I'll never be a lap dog, licking dirty feet,
A sleek dog, a meek dog, cringing for my meat.
Not for me the fireside, the well-filled plate,
But shut door and sharp stone and cuff and kick and
hate.

Not for me the other dogs, running by my side,
Some have run a short while, but none of them would
bide.
O mine is still the lone trail, the hard trail, the best,
Wide wind and wild stars and the hunger of the quest.

FRANCIS BRET HARTE
Coyote, or the Prairie Wolf

ᕋᕐ

Blown out of the prairie in twilight and dew,
Half bold and half timid, yet lazy all through;
Loth ever to leave, and yet fearful to stay,
He limps in the clearing, – an outcast in grey.

A shade on the stubble, a ghost by the wall,
Now leaping, now limping, now risking a fall,
Lop-eared and large jointed, but ever alway
A thoroughly vagabond outcast in grey.

Here, Carlo, old fellow, he's one of your kind, –
Go seek him, and bring him in out of the wind.
What! snarling, my Carlo! so – even dogs may
Deny their own kin in the outcast in grey!

Well, take what you will, – though it be on the sly,
Marauding or begging, – I shall not ask why;
But will call it a dole, just to help on his way
A four-footed friar in orders of grey!

ᕋᕐ

SORLEY MacLEAN
Dogs and Wolves

Across eternity, across its snows
I see my unwritten poems,
I see the spoor of their paws dappling
the untroubled whiteness of the snow:
bristles raging, bloody-tongued,
lean greyhounds and wolves
leaping over the tops of the dykes,
running under the shade of the trees of the wilderness
taking the defile of narrow glens,
making for the steepness of windy mountains;
their baying yell shrieking
across the hard barenesses of the terrible times,
their everlasting barking in my ears,
their onrush seizing my mind:
career of wolves and eerie dogs
swift in pursuit of the quarry,
through the forests without veering,
over the mountain tops without sheering;
the mild mad dogs of poetry,
wolves in chase of beauty,
beauty of soul and face,
a white deer over hills and plains,
the deer of your gentle beloved beauty,
a hunt without halt, without respite.

JO HASLAM
The Dog's Heart

ᐁ

like our own is four chambered
as is the bird's; so far we're the same
as any other mammal, although the bird's
heart beats at five times the rate of ours.

Easy to understand that bird transformed to flame
to raw nerve. No wonder that we dream of flying
and can't deny those tales of loss and change –
maiden into swan; swan dying . . .

But the wolf inside the dog is something different
likewise the human hidden in the wolf.
And though I've dreamed another dog-like animal,
touched the muzzle and the fiery pelt

even as the man inside it stood to shrug it off
I don't see the wolf behind the twitching paw
and eyelid of our own sleeping sheepdog
whose dreams of sticks and rabbit holes

are much closer to earth. But if his subtle nose
discerns the wolf in us he keeps it to himself,
and if it beats at something like the same rate
as ours his canine heart conforms to canine laws

to stay dumb, walk on all fours, be the faithful beast,
like Argos who, when after years of absence
Ulysses returned in the disguise that fooled
everyone else, still recognised the one human.

ᐁ

HOMER

FROM

The Odyssey

TRANSLATED BY
Alexander Pope

When wild Ulysses from his native coasts
Long kept by wars and long by tempest tossed,
Arrived at last, poor, old, disguised, alone,
To all his friends and even his Queen unknown:
Changed as he was with age, and toil and cares
Furrowed his rev'rend face, and white his hairs,
In his own palace forced to ask his bread,
Scorned by those slaves his former bounty fed,
Forgot of all his own domestic crew;
The faithful dog alone his rightful master knew!
Unfed, unhoused, neglected on the clay,
Like an old servant, now cashiered he lay;
Touched with resentment of ungrateful man
And longing to behold his ancient lord again.
Him when he saw – he rose and crawled to meet,
('Twas well he could) and fawned, and kissed his feet,
Seized with dumb joy – then falling by his side,
Owned his returning lord, looked up, and died!

GEORGE CRABBE
Fidelity of the Dog

With eye upraised, his master's looks to scan,
The joy, the solace, and the aid of man;
The rich man's guardian, and the poor man's friend,
The only creature faithful to the end.

[34]

C. F. S.
Dogs

Spaniels are all very well,
But they smell.

Sealyhams deposit white hairs
On the chairs.

Wire-hairs are all right,
But they fight.

(Which also applies to the Irish variety,
Such charming society.)

A Dalmatian is no good, of course,
Without a carriage and horse.

And hounds are nice, but you've got
To have such a lot.

Dachshunds are capital fun,
But slightly Hun.

Very large breeds, such as St Bernards, eat
Quantities of meat,

While very small ones, unhappily
Bark so much and so yappily.

But please don't jump to the conclusion that I dislike
A tyke.

It's simply that I prefer
An honest-to-goodness Cur.

DOROTHY MARGARET STUART
King George's Dalmatian AD 1822

Yellow wheels and red wheels, wheels that squeak
      and roar,
Big buttons, brown wigs, and many capes of buff . . .
Someone's bound for Sussex in a coach-and-four;
    And, when the long whips crack,
      Running at the back
       Barks the swift Dalmatian
Whose spots are seven score.

White dust and grey dust, fleeting tree and tower,
Brass horns and copper horns blowing loud and bluff,
Someone's bound for Sussex at eleven miles an hour;
    And, when the long horns blow
    From the dust below
      Barks the swift Dalmatian
Tongued like an apple-flower.

Big domes and little domes, donkey-carts that jog,
High stocks and low pumps and incomparable snuff,
Someone strolls at Brighton, not *very* much incog.;
    And, panting on the grass,
    In his collar bossed with brass,
      Lies the swift Dalmatian,
The King's plum-pudding dog.

[36]

HENRY LAWSON
Dogs of War

Comes the British bulldog first – solid as a log –
He's so ugly in repose that he's a handsome dog;
Full of mild benevolence as his years increase;
Silent as a china dog on the mantelpiece.
    Rub his sides and point his nose,
    Click your tongue and in he goes,
    To the thick of Britain's foes –
    Enemies behind him close –
    (Silence for a while).

Comes a very different dog – tell him at a glance.
Clipped and trimmed and frilled all round, dandy dog
         of France
(Always was a dandy dog, no matter what his age);
Now his every hair and frill is stiff as wire with rage.
        Rub his sides and point his nose,
        Click your tongue and in he goes,
        While behind him France's foes
        Reel and surge and pack and close.

Next comes Belgium's market-dog – hard to realize –
Go-cart dog and barrow dog; he's a great surprise.
Dog that never hurt a cat, did no person harm;
Friendly, kindly, round, and fat as a Johnny Darm.
        Rub his sides and point his nose,
        Click your tongue and in he goes,
        At the flank of Belgium's foes
        Who could *not* behind him close.

Next comes Servia's mongrel pup – mongrel dogs can
         fight;
Up or down, or down or up, whether wrong or right.
He was mad the other day – he is mad today,
Hustling round and raising dust in his backyard way.
        Rub his sides and point his nose,
        Click your tongue and in he goes,
        'Twixt the legs of Servia's foes,
        Biting tails and rearmost toes.

There are various terrier dogs mixed up in the scrap,
Much too small for us to see, much too mad to yap.
Each one, on his frantic own, heard the row
         commence,

Tore with tooth and claw a hole in the backyard
            fence.
        No one called, but in they go,
        Dogs with many a nameless woe,
        Tripping up their common foe –
        (Uproar for a while).

From the snows of Canada, dragging box and bale,
Comes the sledge-dog toiling on, sore-foot from the
            trail.
He'll be useful in the trench, when the nose is blue –
Winter dog that knows the French and the English
            too.
        Rub his sides and point his nose,
        Click your tongue and in he goes,
        At his father's country's foes,
        And his mother's country's foes.

See, there comes to sunny France a dog that runs by
            sight,
Lean and yellow, sharp of nose, long of leg and light,
Silent and bloodthirsty, too; Distance in his eyes,
Leaping high to gain his view, the kangaroo-dog flies!
        Rub his sides and point his nose,
        Click your tongue and up he goes,
        Lands amongst his country's foes –
        And his country's country's foes;
        While they sway and while they close –
        (Silence for a while).

෴

CHRISTOPHER SMART
The Bulldog

Well of all dogs it stands confess'd
Your English bulldogs are the best;
I say it and will set my hand to it;
Camden records it, and I'll stand to it.

WILL OGILVIE
Dandie Dinmonts

༂

Pepper or Mustard – what's the odds?
    Valiant, varmint, lithe and low,
These were the hounds that the wise old gods
    Took to their hunting an aeon ago;
These when the wild boar stamped and stood,
    These when the gaunt wolf snapped at bay,
Grim and relentless, rash and rude,
    Went for the throat in the Dandie way.

Deep in the slope of that dome-like head,
    Under that top-knot crimped and curled,
Surely the fighting fire was fed
    Before the fires were cool in the world;
Surely 'twas these that the cave-men kept,
    Comrades in hunting, sport and war,
Sharing the shelves where their masters slept,
    Tearing the bones that their masters tore.

No? – Well, have it the way you please;
    But I'll wager it wasn't a show-ring Fox,
Poodle or Pom or Pekingese
    That bayed the mammoth among the rocks;
But something tousled and tough and blue,
    Lined like a weasel – arch and dip,
Coming up late, as the Dandies do,
    And going right in with the Border grip.

༂

R. J. RICHARDSON
The Kerry Blue
❧

The dog from County Kerry,
   The tousled tyke and grey,
See how he meets the merry
   And tires them all at play;
Yet, though he's raced and tumbled
   With many a mongrel crew,
The proudest shall be humbled
   That slight the Kerry Blue.

His fathers lived by battle
   Where crags and lakes and bogs
And glens of small black cattle
   Had work for bold grey dogs;
Shrill Poms he'll scorn with kindness,
   Gruff Airedales they shall rue,
The day when in their blindness
   They roused the Kerry Blue.

Dark eyes afire for slaughter,
   White teeth to hold and kill
Great otters by the water,
   Big badgers in the hill;
The gamest eighteen-inches
   That ever gripped and slew –
Wise is the foe that flinches
   That flees the Kerry blue!

Ah, pup that came from Kerry,
　　Unfriended and unfed,
To maul my boots and bury
　　Your beef-bones in my bed,
You dream of Munster gorses,
　　But – here your heart shines through –
You let my tame resources
　　Content a Kerry Blue.

❧

[40]

B. A. R.

Pre-War Cruft's

❧

Cold the morning dawns, and bright,
Fetch the dogs, no time to dally,
(We have washed them overnight)
Don't forget your cards and tally.
Just in time to catch our train.
Pogo's scuffling in her hamper,
Bolo's pulling on his chain
Keen to have another scamper.
They'll have time to settle down
Long before we get to town.

Such a happy friendly crew
At Victoria Station early.
Sporting Parsons not a few,
Squires, Keepers, Farmers burly,
Eager dogs and jostling men

Women, too, there are in plenty.
Judging starts at half-past ten,
Can we get there by ten-twenty?
Here's a taxi . . . loudly call
'To the Agricultural Hall!'

Once inside the show we find
Dogs of many breeds and nations.
Terriers of every kind,
Yapping Toys and grave Alsatians
People, too, odd contrasts make;
London girls and country wenches.
Gentlemanly ladies take
Shooting dogs towards their benches.
With a common link between,
Mayfair chats with Bethnal Green.

Buy a catalogue and see,
When your puppy judgement faces,
Who his rivals are to be . . .
What's his class? Ah, here the place is.
Anxiously we scan the page.
He is in a class of seven.
Well, he's hefty for his age,
Chances, I should say, are even.
While we're waiting, let us walk
Through the crowd and hear them talk.

Scraps of conversation fall:–
'I have such a lovely litter!'
'. . . never looked at him *at all*!'
'. . . said my Cocker spaniel bit her!'
'Come and see my puppies soon!'
'Fancy putting *that* dog over . . . !'

'Give about a tablespoon . . . !'
'*Quite* unsound! A *shocking* mover!'
'Isn't it a shameful thing?'
'Labradors have got our ring!'

Camera pressmen everywhere
Round about the place are dotted.
If you're picturesque, beware!
You may find yourself snap-shotted.
There two girls with Samoyeds
Pulling them, wear smiles seraphic.
Coloured 'kerchiefs round their heads,
(See to-morrow's 'Daily Graphic')
Here upon their owner's knees,
Pose a bunch of Pekingese.

Hark! A steward calls aloud,
'Class two-forty, please get ready!'
Take your puppy through the crowd,
Make him stand and keep him steady.
Will he pass among the rest?
(Two are better than I reckoned)
Ah! the judge likes that one best,
Never mind, you've got a second.
Wonder if the winning pup
Will secure the Challenge Cup?

Judging's over. We are free
Through the crowded Hall to wander
Many well-known folk we see
That is Mr Marples yonder.
Here some artists work away
Mr Lodge portrays a setter,
'Excellent' its owners say,
'Really could not have been better.'

Mrs Nelson, busy too,
Paints a well-known Kerry Blue.

This poor Bulldog, far too stout,
Thinks the show a doubtful pleasure.
He can scarcely move about.
Here's a little Golden treasure!
Hard and active some of these,
Others need a course of banting
Soft and flabby, so obese
Every movement sets them panting.
Can you really credit that
Judges like them *quite* so fat?

This Dalmatian Swell has plums
Spotted, like a Christmas pudding.
From the Coaching strain he comes,
He's a champion in the budding.
Silver Wings has beauty rare
See, with red her bench is blazing.
Puppy (with a day to spare)
Her achievement is amazing.
Grand Surprise has borne away
The dog championship to-day.

Almost you can fancy, here,
That the Cairns when grouped together,
Bring a subtle atmosphere
Redolent of hills and heather.
'Moorland,' 'Bracken,' 'Of the Mist,'
'Silver Seaway' and 'Phiona'
(Just to take a random list)
'Glenmohr,' 'Of the West,' and 'Rona'
Prefixes and pedigrees
Teem with magic names like these.

In the Gilbey Hall below
'Frenchies' form a pleasing feature.
This one, Germaine of Silpho
Is a charming little creature,
Champions Thisbe and her son
Watch the moving crowd sedately.
Tachette smiles, for she has won
Quite a lot of prizes lately . . .
L'Entente Polisonne, the pied,
Also looks self-satisfied.

Certain things you must not do
If you mean to take up showing.
Should high honours fall to you,
Keeping your head, refrain from crowing.
Your rejoicing, let me say
Means another person's sorrow,
And your champion dog to-day,
May be V.H.C. to-morrow.
Should the judges all agree
Where would the excitement be?

Every judge should have a skin
Like a rhino's epidermis,
For the time he has is 'thin,'
As the somewhat vulgar term is.
If he's wise he will not mind
How the disappointed chatter.
Most exhibitors are kind,
And the others do not matter.
So our judges do contrive
Many of them, to survive.

Don't believe in all you see.
Sight may sometimes be misleading.

When a pup, supposed to be
Of its charming owner's breeding,
Several special prizes wins,
And you think you've recognized it,
That in fact, its origin's
Not as she has advertised it,
Don't protest or feel aggrieved,
For your eyes have been deceived.

Don't believe in all you smell.
What you take for disinfectant
Sprayed to keep our puppies well,
(For we're ever half expectant
Of the dread Distemper foe)
Is expensive perfume really;
All the papers tell us so.
All reporters state it clearly,
All reporters always do,
So of course it must be true.

When it's whispered at the shows
That a dog we need not mention
Has a coffee-coloured nose,
Till it has received attention,
That a Pom of orange hue
Would not stand the test of water,
Or that snowy hairs once grew
On the chest of 'Darkie Daughter.'
Hairs extracted day by day –
Don't believe a word they say.

Closing time has come at last
No need now to brace your muscles
As in the exciting past
When there were such fearful tussles!

How we did it, goodness knows.
In the crowd we fought so madly,
Trampling on each others toes
While our garments suffer badly
Lucky if we struggled through
Safe and sound, though black and blue.

Home we're rushing in the train,
Dogs and we alike are tired.
Still I hope you'll try again,
For your puppy was admired.
Showing brings you many a friend,
And, if you are persevering,
Profit may with pleasure blend.
Anyhow, the hope is cheering!
Pleasant 'tis when we can say
That we make our kennels pay.

Well, our journey's nearly done,
There are only two more stations.
One more 'Cruft's' has come and gone,
With its triumphs and vexations,
With its thrills of hope and fear,
And we're heartily agreeing
That we'll go again next year,
Our united verdict being
That it was a splendid show
And we *did* enjoy it so!

෴

ROBIN IVY
Dogs

ৎ৯

They were people, those dogs,
Locked up in bodies they could not escape from,
Companions for our childhood days.
Dawn, the elegant Red Setter;
Oonagh, the Irish Wolfhound,
Ill-treated when young
Crated trembling in a railway-siding,
Nervy and anxious, gazing into the distance
On the wide Ham by the Severn
Searching for the slightest movement
Then setting off on a chase;
At night howling mournfully at the moon
From the depths of some dark sorrow.
Diana, the Springer Spaniel,
Floppy-eared and housewifely,
Tracking us down across fields,
A faithful companion who loved to retrieve
Old tennis balls on the lawn.
She was more loving than Gyp,
The snappy yappy terrier who delicately took
Fingers of bread and butter at teatime:
And there was Rudy with his bulging eyes
And pug-like smell who loved to sleep
Under the quilt at the bottom of the bed;
Small in size but great in character,
Determined not to be left behind but to keep up
With the Big Dogs on long walks.
How they loved to romp and hunt

Through the fields in their happy days,
Those dogs.
It was all scent and excitement,
Once putting up a fox and rolling him over,
When he bared his teeth and escaped
Into a ditch to vanish in a spinney.
One dog never went out with us,
That was Bob, the Old English Sheepdog.
And we were told never to touch him.
One day he had tried to jump
The six-foot railings and had been
Spiked through the stomach.
It was evening and Bob could not be found.
When they saw him and called out to him
He gave a wag of his tail and fainted.
He survived but kept to himself,
Shambling about like an old sea captain
Or lying across the steps of the porch
Discouraging the postman from
Delivering the mail

It was sad when companions died
And when Diana became too stiff
To come out with us, sitting by the door
Of the tack-room with a frown on her face
As we set out on another long expedition
To the common where the gorse gleamed gold
And the long rides invited
Many more carefree days under a wide sky
To dream about in the evening
Twitching by the hearth.

ALEXANDER POPE
Spaniel

❧

When milder autumn summer's heat succeeds,
  And in the new shorn field the partridge feeds,
Before his lord the ready spaniel bounds,
  Panting with hope he tries the furrowed grounds,
But when the tainted gales the game betray,
  Couched close he lies and meditates the prey.

❧

[43]

ROBERT HERRICK
Upon his Spaniel Tracie

❧

Now thou art dead. No eye shall ever see
For shape and service spaniel like to thee.
This shall my love do. Give thy sad death one
Tear, that deserves of me a million.

❧

WILLIAM COWPER
Epitaph on Fop

A Dog belonging to Lady Throckmorton

Though once a puppy, and Fop by name,
Here moulders one whose bones some honour claim;
No sycophant, although of spaniel race!
And though no hound, a martyr to the chase!
Ye squirrels, rabbits, leverets, rejoice!
Your haunts no longer echo to his voice;
This record of his fate exulting view,
He died worn out with vain pursuit of you.
'Yes' – the indignant shade of Fop replies –
'And worn with vain pursuit, man also dies.'

E. V. LUCAS

The Pekinese

The Pekinese
Adore their ease
And slumber like the dead;
In comfort curled
They view the world
As one unending bed.

CLARISSE ALCOCK
Peggy, the Toy Pomeranian

Oh no, you need not worry any more
About her dirty paws upon the floor,
The polish will remain a spotless thing,
The hearthrug never want remodelling.

There'll be no need to shake the cushions up,
Or place your coffee saucer with the cup
For safety on the shelf, in case by chance
'Tis broken by your little friend's advance.

You'll no more have to make the evening meal,
Sweep the mess and crumbs up when you feel
That every thing's a bother, and a pet
Makes such a lot of trouble, work and fret.

Your garden now will show no sign at all
That somewhere a small blue rubber ball
Is safely hidden, more than likely where
The bulbs are set for blossoming next year.

Never again the tiny pattering feet
Will hurry up the polished hall to greet
And give you joyous welcome, when you come
A weary traveller anxious to be home.

Oh no! these things won't fuss you any more,
No little footprints now will soil the floor,
No yapping to annoy you when you come –
BUT OH! your house will be no more a home.

[47]

W. SOMERVILLE
FROM
The Bloodhound

Soon the sagacious brute, his curling tail
Flourished in air, low bending, plies around
His busy nose, the steaming vapour snuffs
Inquisitive, nor leaves one turf untried,
Till, conscious of the recent stains, his heart
Beats quick. His snuffing nose, his active tail,
Attest his joy. Then, with deep opening mouth,

That makes the welkin tremble, he proclaims
Th' audacious felon. Foot by foot he marks
His winding way. Over the watery ford
Dry sandy heaths, and stony barren hills,
Unerring he pursues, till at the cot
Arrived, and, seizing by his guilty throat
The caitiff vile, redeems the captive prey.

[48]

RUTH PITTER
Digdog

Inspired by the English of a Belgian hotel-keeper.
'Ze ladies, zey lof ze Griffon Bruxellois; mais moi,
je préfére ze English digdog! ze brave renardearther.'
i.e. fox-terrier.

Rooting in packingcase of
dirty straw hurling
lumps of it overboard moaning desire
moaning desire of vermin lovely rat
ineffable mouse attar of felicity
BUT there is nothing
nothing but dirt and darkness
but strawdirt chaffdust smellillusion ALAS.
BRAVE CHIEN ANGLAIS
NOBLE RENARDEARTHER
DIGDOG

Alas I also
root in earth desiring
something for nothing digging down to peace.
Follow the mole and not the lark
bet with the bloke who knows
peace lies there whence from the dark
arise the lily and the rose,
peace rains down in rivers of gold
and there great nuggets of sleep
wait for the seeker ever been sold
sit on your tail and weep
for there is nothing

nothing but dust and darkness
but strawdirt chaffdust smellillusion ALAS.
LACHE ESPRIT ANGLAIS
POLTRON DE RENARDEARTHER
DIGDOG

JOHN GAY
Mastiff

A mastiff of true English blood
Loved fighting better than his food;
He gloried in his limping pace,
The scars of honour seamed his face;
In every limb a gash appears,
And frequent fights retrenched his ears.

WILLIAM COWPER
An Epitaph

Here lies one who never drew
Blood himself, yet many slew;
Gave the gun its aim, and figure
Made in field, yet ne'er pulled trigger.
Armèd men have gladly made
Him their guide, and him obeyed;
At his signified desire,
Would advance, present and fire –
Stout he was, and large of limb,
Scores have fled at sight of him;
And to all this fame he rose
Only following his nose.
Neptune was he called, not he
Who controls the boisterous sea,
But of happier command,
Neptune of the furrowed land;
And, your wonder vain to shorten,
Pointer to Sir John Throckmorton.

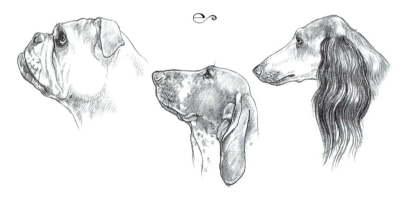

JOHN GAY
The Pointer

The subtle dog, now with sagacious nose,
Scours through the field and snuffs each breeze that
    blows,
Against the wind he takes his prudent way,
While the strong gale directs him to the prey;
Now the warm scent assures the covey near,
He treads with caution, and he points with fear;
Then lest some sentry foul his fraud descry,
And bid his fellows from the danger fly,
Close to the ground in expectation lies,
Till in the snare the fluttering covey rise.

[52]

LORD GRENVILLE
Tippo. A Newfoundland Dog

Here, stranger, pause, nor view with scornful eyes
The stone which marks where faithful Tippo lies.
Freely kind Nature gave each liberal grace,
Which most ennobles and exalts our race,
Excelling strength and beauty joined in me
Ingenious worth and firm fidelity.
Nor shame I to have borne a tyrant's name,
So far unlike to his my spotless fame.

Cast by a fatal storm on Tenby's coast
Reckless of life I wailed my master lost.
Whom long contending with the o'erwhelming wave
In vain with fruitless love I strove to save.
I, only I, alas! surviving bore
His dying trust, his tablets to the shore.
Kind welcome from the Belgian race I found,
Who, once in times remote, to British ground
Strangers like me came from a foreign strand.
I loved at large along the extended sand
To roam, and oft beneath the swelling wave,
Though known so fatal once, my limbs to lave;
Or join the children in their summer play,
First in their sports, companion of their way.
Thus while from many a hand a meal I sought,
Winter and age had certain misery brought;
But Fortune smiled, a safe and blessed abode
A new-found master's generous love bestowed;
And midst these shades, where smiling flowerets
    bloom
Gave me a happy life and honoured tomb.

LORD BYRON
To Boatswain

When some proud son of man returns to earth,
Unknown to glory, but upheld by birth,
The sculptor's art exhausts the pomp and woe,
And storied urns record who rest below;
When all is done, upon the tomb is seen,
Not what he was, but what he should have been:
But the poor dog, in life the firmest friend,
The first to welcome, foremost to defend,
Whose honest heart is still his master's own,
Who labours, fights, lives, breathes for him alone,
Unhonour'd falls, unnoticed all his worth,
Denied in heaven the soul he held on earth:
While man, vain insect! hopes to be forgiven,
And claims himself a sole exclusive heaven.
Oh, man! thou feeble tenant of an hour,
Debased by slavery, or corrupt by power,
Who knows thee well must quit thee with distrust,
Degraded mass of animated dust!
Thy love is lust, thy friendship all a cheat,
Thy smiles hypocrisy, thy words deceit!
By nature vile, ennobled but by name,
Each kindred brute might bid thee blush for shame.
Ye! who perchance behold this simple urn,
Pass on – it honours none you wish to mourn,
To mark a friend's remains these stones arise;
I never knew but one – and here he lies.

[54]

EARL OF ELDON
Epitaph on a Favourite Newfoundland

You who wander hither,
Pass not unheeded
The spot where poor Caesar
Is deposited.

To his rank among created beings
The power of reasoning is denied!
Caesar manifested joy
For days before his master
Arrived at Encombe;
Caesar manifested grief
For days before his master left it.
What name shall be given
To that faculty
Which thus made expectation
A source of joy,
Which thus made expectation
A source of grief?

JULIAN GRENFELL
To a Black Greyhound

Shining black in the shining light,
  Inky black in the golden sun,
Graceful as the swallow's flight,
  Light as swallow, wingèd one.
Swift as driven hurricane –
  Double-sinewed stretch and spring,
Muffled thud of flying feet,
  See the black dog galloping,
  Hear his wild foot-beat.

See him lie when the day is dead,
  Black curves curled on the boarded floor,
Sleepy eyes, my sleepy-head –
  Eyes that were aflame before.
Gentle now, they burn no more;
  Gentle now and softly warm,

With the fire that made them bright
    Hidden – as when after storm
    Softly falls the night.

God of speed, who makes the fire –
    God of Peace, who lulls the same –
God who gives the fierce desire,
    Lust for blood as fierce as flame –
God who stands in Pity's name –
    Many may ye be or less,
Ye who rule the earth and sun:
    Gods of strength and gentleness,
    Ye are ever one.

[56]

ANONYMOUS
Old Adage on Grey-hounds

ꜱ

If you will have a good tike,
Of which there are few like,
He must be headed like a snake,
Neckt like a Drake,
Backt like a Beam,
Sided like a Bream,
Tayled like a Rat
And footed like a Cat.

ꜱ

[57]

ROB EVANS
For a Lurcher

ꜱ

Did Freya run like the wind? That is not the right
way to describe it. For the wind has no bounding
joy, it would not race through the morning-bright
dewed grass of the downs with a glad heart pounding.
No, she ran *in* the wind, shadowing the weaving
    dance
of the sprung hare with supple, sinewed elegance.

She was my own brindled beauty, my wilful thief,
casual taker of unconsidered trifles, pies,

~ 81 ~

cream cakes and even Sunday joints of beef;
any unguarded food would catch those guileless eyes.
Harsh words had no effect. That narrow head was
    built
for speed and far too full of love to harbour guilt.

She was the lightning flash made flesh and yet time
    caught her.
Proving the greater thief, it took away her grace,
her fire, and slowed that hunting heart. It brought her
wasted limbs and forced her to a walking pace.
The last days were spent in sleep. Now she is dead
but she still runs in the wind, and in my head.

[58]

PATRICK CHALMERS
The New Anubis

All along the moorland road a caravan there comes
Where the piping curlew whistles and the brown snipe
    drums;
    And a long lean dog
    At a sling jig-jog,
A poacher to his eyelids, as all the lurcher clan,
Follows silent as a shadow, and clever as a man.

His master on the splash-board, oh, of ancient race
    he is;
He came down out of Egypt, as did all the Romanys;
    With the hard hawk face

Of an old king race,
His hair is black and snaky, and his cheek is brown
        as tea,
And pyramids and poacher-dogs are made by such
        as he.
Now the dog he looks as solemn as the beak upon the
        bench,
– he'll pounce and pick a hare up, and he'll kill it
        with a wrench,

Or he'll sneak around a rick
And bring back a turkey chick;
And you'll wonder how they got him all his cock-a-
leerie fakes.
Well, his master comes of people who turn walking
sticks to snakes!

There was once a god in Egypt, when the gods they
first began,
With the muzzle of a lurcher on the body of a man;
But the Pharaoh of to-day
He has changed the ancient way,
And has found him a familiar by his caravan to jog
With the head piece of a Solomon, the body of a dog!

[59]

ANONYMOUS

Irish Wolf Hound

An eye of sloe, with ear not low,
With horse's breast, with depth of chest,
With breadth of loin, and curve in groin,
And nape set far behind the head –
Such were the dogs that Fingal bred.

[60]

LESLIE NORRIS
Deerhound

There are no deerhounds in Wales –
Or perhaps one; in Cardiff, loping
On an elegant lead in Llandaff Fields,
Exotic in Queen Street, posing
For photographs. But there are
No true deerhounds. Our fat corgis
Sit irritably in English country houses,
Our loyal collies starve
Behind the doors of roadless farms.

We parade our terriers. Square
And bristling, the brisk wire-
Haired fox terrier, the Welsh terrier
Indigenous black and tan, thin
Scars on head and legs, like a collier,
We like these dogs. I knew one
Curl herself over a drunk man's heart,
On a moor filling with blizzard
They grin at death with their teeth.

I would have a deerhound coloured
Slippery as charcoal, running
Tactfully at the edge of eyesight,
Soft as dust after his great quarry.
Once, back of the ruined hills, I saw
A fabulous hare living on grass
Too small for sheep, thrusting,
Through coal-spoil. He leapt
In my sleep for months.

With such small deer my hound
Would not soil his slobber.
In darkness, on the edge of terror,
He would run loose, he would run loose and
Noiseless. Black as nightfur, kicking
Into the black, what antlered
Game he would rip at, what
Terrible beasts drag back
Alive for my keeping.

e

NORMAN MacCAIG
Praise of a Collie

She was a small dog, neat and fluid –
Even her conversation was tiny;
She greeted you with *bow* never *bow-wow*.

Her sons stood monumentally over her
But did what she told them. Each grew grizzled
Till it seemed he was his own mother's grandfather.

Once, gathering sheep on a showery day,
I remarked how dry she was. Pollóchan said, 'Ah,
It would take a very accurate drop to hit our Lassie.'

And her tact – and tactics! When the sheep bolted
In an unforeseen direction, over the skyline
Came – who but Lassie, and not even panting.

She sailed in the dinghy like a proper sea-dog.
Where's a burn? – she's first on the other side.
She flowed through fences like a piece of black wind.

But suddenly she was old and sick and crippled. . .
I grieved for Pollóchan when he took her a stroll
And put his gun to the back of her head.

[62]

THOMAS HARDY
The Mongrel

In Havenpool Harbour the ebb was strong,
And a man with a dog drew near and hung,
And taxpaying day was coming along,
 So the mongrel had to be drowned.
The man threw a stick from the paved wharf-side
Into the midst of the ebbing tide,
And the dog jumped after with ardent pride
 To bring the stick aground.

But no: the steady suck of the flood
To seaward needed, to be withstood,
More than the strength of mongrelhood
 To fight its treacherous trend.

So, swimming for life with desperate will,
The struggler with all his natant skill
Kept buoyant in front of his master, still
    There standing to wait the end.

The loving eyes of the dog inclined
To the man he held as a god enshrined,
With no suspicion in his mind
    That this had all been meant.
Till the effort not to drift from shore
Of his little legs grew slower and slower,
And, the tide still outing with brookless power,
    Outward the dog, too, went.

Just ere his sinking what does one see
Break on the face of that devotee?
A wakening to the treachery
    He had loved with love so blind?
The faith that had shone in that mongrel's eye
That his owner would save him by and by
Turned to much like a curse as he sank to die,
    And a loathing of mankind.

W. H. DAVIES
A Dog's Grave

My dog lies dead and buried here,
  My little Pet for five sweet years.
As I stand here, beside her grave,
  With eyes gone dim, and blind with tears –
I see it rising up and down,
As though she lay in a sleeping-gown.

Forgive me, Pet, that half these tears,
  Which make my eyes go dim and blind,
Should come from thoughts of love betrayed,
  When I had trust in my own kind:
And Christ forgive this living breath
That links such lives with my dog's death!

When I was once a wandering man,
  And walked at midnight, all alone –
A friendly dog, that offered love,
  Was threatened with a stone.

'Go, go,' I said, 'and find a man
  Who has a home to call his own;
Who, with a luckier hand than mine,
  Can find his dog a bone.'

But times are changed, and this pet dog
  Knows nothing of a life that's gone –
Of how a dog that offered love
  Was threatened with a stone.

SIR EDWIN ARNOLD
The Pardon

High noon it was, and the hot Khamseen's breath
Blew from the desert sands and parched the town.
The crows gasped; and the kine went up and down
With lolling tongues; the camels moaned; a crowd
Pressed with their pitchers, wrangling high and loud
About the tank; and one dog by a well
Nigh dead with thirst, lay where he yelped and fell
Glaring upon the water out of reach
And praying succour in a silent speech,
So piteous were its eyes. Which, when she saw,
This woman from her foot her shoe did draw
Albeit death-sorrowful; and looping up
The long silk of her girdle, made a cap
Of the heel's hollow, and thus let it sink
Until it touched the cool black water's brink;
So filled th'embroidered shoe, and gave a draught
To the spent beast, which whined and fawned and
    quaffed
Her kind gift to the dregs; next licked her hand
With such glad looks that all might understand
He held his life from her; then at her feet
He followed close all down the cruel street,
Her one friend in that city.
                  But the King,
Riding within his litter, marked the thing,
And how the woman on her way to die,
Had such compassion for the misery
Of that parched hound: 'Take off her chain and place

The veil once more above the sinner's face,
And lead her to her house in peace!' he said.
'The law is that the people stone thee dead,
For that which thou hast wrought; but there is come,
Fawning around thy feet, a witness dumb,
Not heard upon thy trial; this brute beast
Testifies for thee, sister! whose weak breast
Death could not make ungentle. I hold rule
In Allah's stead, who is the Merciful,
And hope for Mercy; therefore go thou free –
I dare not show less pity unto thee.'

[65]

GEOFFREY DEARMER
The Turkish Trench Dog

Night held me as I crawled and scrambled near
The Turkish lines. Above, the mocking stars
Silver the curving parapet, and clear
Cloud-latticed beams o'erflecked the land with bars;
I, crouching, lay between
Tense-listening armies, peering through the night,
Twin giants bound by tentacles unseen.
Here in dim-shadowed light
I saw him, as a sudden movement turned
His eyes towards me, glowing eyes that burned
A moment ere his snuffling muzzle found
My trail; and then as serpents mesmerise
He chained me with those unrelenting eyes,

That muscle-sliding rhythm, knit and bound
In spare-limbed symmetry, those perfect jaws
And soft-approaching pitter-patter paws.
Nearer and nearer like a wolf he crept –
That moment had my swift revolver leapt –
But terror seized me, terror born of shame
Brought flooding revelation. For he came
As one who offers comradeship deserved,
An open ally of the human race,
And sniffing at my prostrate form unnerved
He licked my face!

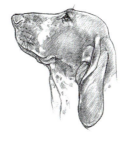

[66]

ANONYMOUS
Worship

How that dog
Loves that man;
He's her god,
She's his slave.

RUDYARD KIPLING
Thy Servant

∾

Master, this is Thy Servant. He is rising eight weeks
    old.
He is mainly Head and Tummy. His legs are
    uncontrolled.
But Thou hast forgiven his ugliness, and settled him
    on Thy knee . . .
Art Thou content with Thy servant? He is *very* comfy
    with Thee.

Master, behold a Sinner! He hath committed a wrong.
He hath defiled Thy Premises through being kept in
    too long.
Wherefore his nose has been rubbed in the dirt, and
    his self-respect has been bruised.
Master, pardon Thy Sinner, and see he is properly
    loosed.

Master – again Thy sinner! This that was once Thy
    Shoe,
He hath found and taken and carried aside, as fitting
    matter to chew.
Now there is neither blacking nor tongue, and the
    Housemaid has us in tow.
Master, remember Thy Servant is young, and tell her
    to let him go!

Master, pity Thy Servant! He is deaf and three parts
    blind.

He cannot catch Thy Commandments. He cannot
read Thy Mind.
Oh, leave him not in his loneliness; nor make him that
kitten's scorn.
He hath had none other God than Thee since the year
that he was born.

Lord, look down on Thy Servant! Bad things have
come to pass.
There is no heat in the midday sun, nor health in the
wayside grass.
His bones are full of an old disease – his torments run
and increase.
Lord, make haste with Thy Lightnings and grant him
a quick release!

KATHLEEN BARROW
Any Dog

No one goes softly if by chance he's ill
Few hesitate to push him from a chair,
Or hate to eat because he's standing there
All shining eyes and hope and wagging tail!
And rarely in the storm or evening chill
Do we relent and take him out to play,
Because he's waited for his treat all day
With perfect trust that we will never fail.
And hour by hour he'll wait our coming still,
His welcome's just the same – without alloy,
As though his very heart would break with joy,
As though without us, sun and moon would pale.

And sometimes quite apart from what we will,
But occupied perhaps with this or that,
We quite forget to give him word or pat,
So that his rapture seems without avail!

And when at last there comes the dreaded break,
Someone who never owned a dog or cat
Will smile and say, 'Rather a fuss to make –
And not a very handsome dog at that!'

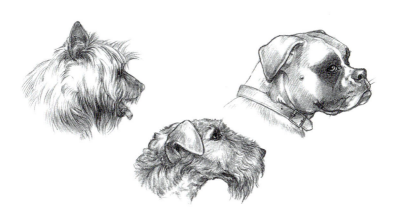

[69]

ELEANOR FARJEON
Bliss

Let me fetch sticks,
Let me fetch stones,
Throw me your bones
Teach me your tricks.

When you go ride
Let me go run
You in the sun,
Me at your side;

When you go swim
Let me go too
Both lost in blue
Up to the brim;

Let me do this,
Let me do that –
What you are at
That is my bliss.

∼

WALTER DE LA MARE
Tom's Little Dog

Tom told his dog called Tim to beg,
And up at once he sat,
His two clear amber eyes fixed fast,
His haunches on his mat.

Tom poised a lump of sugar on
His nose; then, 'Trust!' says he;
Stiff as a guardsman sat his Tim,
Never a hair stirred he.

'Paid for!' says Tom; and in a trice
Up jerked that moist black nose;
A snap of teeth, a crunch, a munch,
And down the sugar goes!

[71]

LES BARKER
Stay, Go and Fetch

I'd always wanted a dog
So one day I took in a stray.
He didn't want to leave me
And so I called him Stay.

I knew it was a mistake
The first time I told Stay to go.
'Go, Stay,' and I pointed.
Did Stay go? No.

'Go, Stay,' I said; and he started;
He was going . . . then he was not;
He looked at me, sad and confused,
And his two big eyes said 'What?'

I threw him a stick; I said 'Fetch, Stay.'
He started and stopped all in one;
I never got round to 'Come here, Stay.'
Stay couldn't come; he'd not gone.

He wanted to please, but he couldn't;
I spoke, but he just didn't know;
So I got him a spaniel for company.
I shouldn't have called it Go.

I said 'Stay, Go,' and Go'd stay a second
Then both Stay and Go were away
And I had to shout 'Come here, Stay and Go.'
They were coming and going all day.

I said 'Stay, Go and Stay.' I tried 'Go, Stay and Go.'
Nothing seemed to get through;
It's not that they were both saying 'No.'
They were both saying 'Does he mean you?'

It's all very well in the park,
But what if we're stood at the kerb?
Two lost souls in the dark;
Which bloody one is the verb?

I've got them a new friend now;
I found him, a poor starving wretch;
I hope they'll be happy together;
Go and Stay; come and meet Fetch.

RALPH WOTHERSPOON
My Dumb Friends

My home is a haven for one who enjoys
The clamour of children and ear-splitting noise
From a number of dogs who are always about,
And who want to come in and, once in, to go out.
Whenever I settle to read by the fire,
Some dog will develop an urge to retire,
And I'm constantly opening and shutting the door
For a dog to depart or, as mentioned before,
For a dog to arrive who, politely admitted,
Will make a bee-line for the chair I've just quitted.
Our friends may be dumb, but my house is a riot,
Where I cannot sit still and can never be quiet.

[73]

ALAN ROSS
Dim Dog

He imagines he's invisible,
Head buried in cushions, tail
Splayed like a palm tree,
Impolite end aiming at me.

Dim dog, just because *he*
Is unable to see *me*,

He thinks he's been clever,
Nose twitching, as if scenting a river.

It's only a game though, a lark,
And soon, tiring of the dark,
He swivels, muzzle soft felt,
Butterscotch eyes beginning to melt.

&

[74]

ALLAN AHLBERG
Dog in the Playground
&

Dog in the playground
Suddenly there.
Smile on his face,
Tail in the air.

Dog in the playground
Bit of a fuss:
I know that dog –
Lives next to us!

Dog in the playground:
Oh, no he don't.
He'll come with me,
You see if he won't.

The word gets round;
The crowd gets bigger.
His name's Bob.
It ain't – it's Trigger.

They call him Archie!
They call him Frank!
Lives by the Fish Shop!
Lives up the Bank!
Who told you that?
Pipe down! Shut up!
I know that dog
Since he was a pup.

Dog in the playground:
We'll catch him, Miss.
Leave it to us.
Just watch this!

Dog in the playground
What a to-do!
Thirty-five children,
Caretaker too,
Chasing the dog,
Chasing each other.
I know that dog –
He's our dog's brother!

[75]

JACK PRELUTSKY
Hello! How are You? I am Fine!

Hello! How are you? I am fine!
Is all my dog will say.
He's probably repeated it
A thousand times to-day.

He doesn't bark his normal bark,
He doesn't even whine
He only drones the same Hello
How are you? I am fine.
Hello! How are you? I am fine!
His message doesn't change,
It's gotten quite monotonous
And just a trifle strange.
Hello! How are you? I am fine!
It makes the neighbours stare
They're unaware that yesterday
He ate my talking bear.

[76]

ANONYMOUS
My Little Dog

I'll never hurt my little dog
But stroke and pat his head;
I like to see him wag his tail
I like to see him fed.

Poor little thing, how very good
And very useful too;
For do you know that he will mind
What he is bid to do?

Then I will never hurt my dog
And never give him pain
But treat him kindly every day
And he'll love me again.

FRANCES CORNFORD
A Child's Dream

I had a little dog, and my dog was very small;
He licked me in the face, and he answered to my call;
Of all the treasures that were mine, I loved him most
    of all.

His nose was fresh as morning dew and blacker than
    the night;
I thought that it could even snuff the shadows and the
    light;
And his tail he held bravely, like a banner in a fight.

His body covered thick with hair was very good to
    smell;
His little stomach underneath was pink as any shell;
And I loved him and honoured him more than words
    can tell.

We ran out in the morning, both of us, to play.
Up and down across the fields for all the sunny day;
But he ran so swiftly – he ran right away.

I looked for him, I called him, entreatingly. Alas,
The dandelions could not speak, though they had seen
    him pass,
And nowhere was his waving tail among the waving
    grass.

I called him in a thousand ways and yet he did not
    come;
The pathways and the hedges were horrible and
    dumb.
I prayed to God, who never heard. My desperate soul
    grew numb.

The sun sank low. I ran; I prayed 'If God has not the
    power
To find him, let me die. I cannot bear another hour.'
When suddenly I came upon a great yellow flower.

And all among its petals, such was Heaven's grace,
In that golden hour, in that golden place,
All among its petals, was his hairy face.

HESTER DUNLOP
Daughter

Whistling
Blackberry smudged fingers.
Daisy chain happiness.
Twisting down gritstone road.

Racing after her tail wagging dog
who is ignorant of sticks
and leaves squirtable traces
of amber on stone

unlocking secret glints
of diamonds.
Temporary jewels.
A rainbow.

A grey thundercloud.
Freckles
bursting into song
across a stave of nose.

THORA STOVELL
Binkie and Me

Binkie and me in the twilight time
Creep up the stairs
Me with my gun and Binks with his growl
Hunting bears.

Oh, the loveliest time in the day for me
Is when we two creep up the stairs;
Me with my gun and Binks with his growl
Hunting bears.

SPIKE MILLIGAN
My Boyhood Dog

Boxer, my Boxer,
where do you lie?
Somewhere under
a Poona sky.
Ah! my canine,
total joy
you were to me
when as a boy
we coursed the wind

and ran the while,
no end in sight,
mile after mile.
I was to you
and you to me
locked in a bond
eternally.
They never told me
when you died
to spare me pain
in case I cried.
So then to
those adult fears
denied you then,
my childhood tears.

RICHARD WILBUR
The Pardon

My dog lay dead five days without a grave
In the thick summer, hid in a clump of pine
And a jungle of grass and honeysuckle-vine.
I who had loved him while he kept alive

Went only close enough to where he was
To sniff the heavy honeysuckle-smell
Twined with another odor heavier still
And hear the flies' intolerable buzz.

Well, I was ten and very much afraid.
In my kind world the dead were out of range
And I could not forgive the sad or strange
In beast or man. My father took the spade

And buried him. Last night I saw the grass
Slowly divide (it was the same scene
But now it glowed a fierce and mortal green)
And saw the dog emerging. I confess

I felt afraid again, but still he came
In the carnal sun, clothed in a hymn of flies,
And death was breeding in his lively eyes.
I started in to cry and call his name,

Asking forgiveness of his tongueless head.
. . . I dreamt the past was never past redeeming:
But whether this was false or honest dreaming
I beg death's pardon now. And mourn the dead.

JAMES WRIGHT
On the Skeleton of a Hound

Nightfall, that saw the morning-glories float
Tendril and string against the crumbling wall,
Nurses him now, his skeleton for grief,
His locks for comfort curled among the leaf.
Shuttles of moonlight weave his shadow tall,
Milkweed and dew flow upward to his throat.
Now catbird feathers plume the apple mound,
And starlings drowse to winter up the ground.
Thickened away from speech by fear, I move
Around the body. Over his forepaws, steep
Declivities darken down the moonlight now
And the long throat that bayed a year ago
Declines from summer. Flies would love to leap
Between his eyes and hum away the space
Between the ears, the hollow where a hare
Could hide; another jealous dog would tumble
The bones apart, angry, the shining crumble
Of a great body gleaming in the air;
Quivering pigeons foul his broken face.
I can imagine men who search the earth
For handy resurrections, overturn
The body of a beetle in its grave;
Whispering men digging for gods might delve
A pocket for these bones, then slowly burn
Twigs in the leaves, pray for another birth.

But I will turn my face away from this
Ruin of summer, collapse of fur and bone.

For once a white hare huddled up the grass,
The sparrows flocked away to see the race.
I stood on darkness, clinging to a stone,
I saw the two leaping alive on ice,
On earth, on leaf, humus and withered vine:
The rabbit splendid in a shroud of shade,
The dog carved on the sunlight, on the air,
Fierce and magnificent his rippled hair,
The cockleburrs shaking around his head.
Then, suddenly, the hare leaped beyond pain
Out of the open meadow, and the hound
Followed the voiceless dancer to the moon,
To dark, to death, to other meadows where
Singing young women dance around a fire,
Where love reveres the living. I alone
Scatter this hulk about the dampened ground;
And while the moon rises beyond me, throw
The ribs and spine out of their perfect shape.
For a last charm to the dead, I lift the skull
And toss it over the maples like a ball.
Strewn to the woods, now may that spirit sleep
That flamed over the ground a year ago.
I know the mole will heave a shinbone over,
The earthworm snuggle for a nap on paws,
The honest bees build honey in the head;
The earth knows how to handle the great dead
Who lived the body out, and broke its laws,
Knocked down a fence, tore up a field of clover.

WILLIAM WORDSWORTH
To the Memory of Little Music

Lie here, without a record of thy worth,
Beneath a covering of the common earth!
It is not for unwillingness to praise,
Or want of love, that here no stone we raise;
More thou deserv'st; but *this* man gives to man,
Brother to brother, *this* is all we can.
Yet they to whom thy virtues made thee dear
Shall find thee through all changes of the year;
This oak points out thy grave; the silent tree
Will gladly stand, a monument of thee.

We grieved for thee and wished thy end were past;
And willingly have laid thee here at last:
For thou hadst lived till everything that cheers
In thee had yielded to the weight of years;
Extreme old age had wasted thee away,
And left thee but a glimmering of the day;
Thy ears were deaf, and feeble were thy knees –
I saw thee stagger in the summer breeze,
Too weak to stand against its sportive breath,
And ready for the gentlest stroke of death.
It came, and we were glad; yet tears were shed;
Both man and woman wept when thou wert dead;
Not only for a thousand thoughts that were
Old household thoughts in which thou hadst thy
    share,
But for some precious boons vouchsafed to thee
Found scarcely anywhere in like degree!

For love that comes wherever life and sense
Are given to God, in thee was most intense;
A chain of heart, a feeling of the mind,
A tender sympathy, which did thee bind
Not only to us men, but to thy kind:
Yea, for thy fellow-brutes in thee we saw,
A soul of love, love's intellectual law: –
Hence, if we wept, it was not done in shame;
Our tears from passion and from reason came,
And therefore shalt thou be an honoured name!

[84]

ANONYMOUS
On a Dog's Grave

From the Greek

You that pass me, do not sneer
  Though a dog be buried here.
Rather think, with tears my lord
  Stored these ashes, graved this word.

THOMAS HARDY
Dead 'Wessex' the Dog to the Household

Do you think of me at all,
    Wistful ones?
Do you think of me at all
    As if nigh?
Do you think of me at all
At the creep of evenfall,
Or when the sky-birds call
    As they fly?

Do you look for me at times,
    Wistful ones?
Do you look for me at times
    Strained and still?
Do you look for me at times,
When the hour for walking chimes,
On that grassy path that climbs
    Up the hill?

You may hear a jump or trot,
    Wistful ones,
You may hear a jump or trot –
    Mine, as 'twere –
You may hear a jump or trot
On the stair or path or plot;
But I shall cause it not,
    Be not there.

Should you call as when I knew you,
    Wistful ones,
Should you call as when I knew you,
    Shared your home;
Should you call as when I knew you,
I shall not turn to view you,
I shall not listen to you,
    Shall not come.

ↄᴗ

[86]

MATTHEW ARNOLD
Geist's Grave

ↄᴗ

Four years! – and didst thou stay above
The ground which hides thee now but four;
And all that life, and all that love,
Were crowded, Geist! into no more?

Only four years those winning ways,
Which make me for thy presence yearn,
Call'd us to pet thee or to praise,
Dear little friend, at every turn?

That loving heart, that patient soul,
Had they indeed no longer span,
To run their course, and reach their goal,
And read their homily to man?

That liquid melancholy eye,
From whose pathetic, soul-fed springs
Seemed surging the Virgilian cry,
The sense of tears in mortal things –

That steadfast mournful strain, consoled
By spirits gloriously gay,
And temper of heroic mould –
What, was four years their whole short day?

Yes, only four! – and not the course
Of all the centuries yet to come,
And not the infinite resource
Of Nature, with her countless sum

Of figures, with her fullness vast
Of new creation evermore,
Can ever quite repeat the past,
Or just thy little self restore.

Stern law of every mortal lot!
Which man, proud man, finds hard to bear,
And builds himself I know not what
Of second life I know not where.

But thou, when struck thine hour to go,
On us, who stood despondent by,
A meek last glance of love didst throw,
And humbly lay thee down to die.

Yet would we keep thee in our heart –
Would fix our favourite on the scene,
Nor let thee utterly depart
And be as if thou ne'er hadst been.

And so there rise these lines of verse
On lips that rarely form them now;
While to each other we rehearse;
Such ways, such arts, such looks hadst thou!

We stroke thy broad brown paws again,
We bid thee to thy vacant chair,
We greet thee by the window-pane,
We hear thy scuffle on the stair.

We see the flaps of thy large ears
Quick raised to ask which way we go;
Crossing the frozen lake, appears
Thy small black figure on the snow!

Not to us only art thou dear
Who mourn thee in thine English home;
Thou hast thine absent master's tear,
Dropt by the far Australian foam.

Thy memory lasts both here and there,
And thou shalt live as long as we,
And after that – thou dost not care!
In us was all the world to thee.

Yet, fondly jealous for thy fame,
Even to a date beyond our own,
We strive to carry down thy name
By mounded turf, and graven stone.

We lay thee, close within our reach,
Here, where the grass is smooth and warm,
Between the holly and the beech,
Where oft we watched thy couchant form,

Asleep, yet lending half an ear
To travellers on the Portsmouth road; –
There build we thee, O guardian dear,
Mark'd with a stone thy last abode!

Then some, who through this garden pass,
When we two, like thyself, are clay,
Shall see thy grave upon the grass,
And stop before the stone, and say:

People who lived here long ago
Did by this stone, it seems, intend
To name for future times to know
The dachshound, Geist, their little friend.

SYDNEY SMITH
Good Nick

Here lies poor Nick, an honest creature,
Of faithful, gentle, courteous nature;
A parlour pet unspoiled by favour,
A pattern of good dog behaviour.
Without a wish, without a dream,
Beyond his home and friends at Cheam.
Contentedly through life he trotted
Along the path that fate allotted;
Till Time, his aged body wearing,
Bereaved him of his sight and hearing,
Then laid them down without a pain
To sleep, and never wake again.

[88]

JONATHAN SWIFT
Epitaph

Of all the dogs arrayed in fur,
Hereunder lies the truest cur.
He knew no tricks, he never flattered:
Nor those he fawned upon bespattered.

[89]

JUDITH ADAMS
Crackers

Crackers worshipped at the creek
Said his prayers sideways
Swimming the current to
catch a stick

Wholehearted
Tail wagging to the
Edge expecting flight
Into sacred waters.

Crackers did not question faith
he believed in life and
the love of workman
The gift of a torn tea cloth

without prejudice. Whatever
interested you, was already
him. In the end

He pulled back up the hill
His lungs breathing a corner
His God gone silent.

Taken home
As if the day
Forgot to arrive and
the Sun had betrayed
the earth.

We lit candles
The Vet came because
he knew Crackers did not want
To live
Half in Prayer

His beloved wind
Barking
in the shadows
of the moon

We chanted the best
we knew
Crackers curled
into the earth . . .

Then the snow came.

⟳

JOE WALKER
The Decision

ᘒ

'Tis not your going that has bruised my heart;
I knew the time was near when we must part.
Nearly twelve years! and life was scarce worth while
For you, too old. I trusted I might smile
If some day I should wake to find that Fate
Had said 'Sleep on,' and I, though desolate,
Might comfort take in thought of you at rest
And strive to murmur 'All is for the best.'
Yes, then I *might* have smiled – but that to me
Was left the verdict, that 'twas my decree
Which sent you forth, you whom I treasured so . . .
This is my torment, this the crushing blow.

ᘒ

[91]

PETER ARTHUR
Liz

ᘒ

She loved me, yes –
or so I thought;
but was it love
or my conceit?
I'll take a chance
and call it love.

Gun-dog?
No, he said,
too highly strung,
untrainable,
have her cheap –
she'll be the last to go.

Not cheap to me;
but nervous, yes –
ran wild in panic
'till she found her
sanctuary
at my side.

Learns well, responds,
obeys, tracks scent
tail high in ecstasy,
checks, points,
looks back, swings round,
head down and – go!

I'd say she shared
herself with me,
knew my moods
marked my voice;
in turn I cared
that she was sick.

As ebbed her life,
I sensed the pain
and marvelled at
her patient,
uncomplaining
stoicism.

When she was set
to die, we laid
her down upon
the lino floor . . .
my hand lay
lightly on her head.

෧෨

[92]

GLYN JONES
Remembering Siani

෧෨

She leaps in sunlight, her grin wicked –
With all the élan of a French forward
She brings down her blue ball,
Her silky butterscotch coat shedding
A shaken-off golden sheen, a nimbus
Of yellow marigold.
    As children,
In our sunlit kitchen, we gazed down,
Enchanted, into the wonder of the newly opened
Tin of golden syrup – so are her eyes,
Golden, not treacly, darker, more amber,
Warm, firm and clear.
    The barmy Welshman who sold her,
A little thing, to us – how could he? –
Was red-haired, short-legged, bandy and long-nosed,
And so, full-grown, was she; grotesque, absurd,
But yet, beyond belief, and utterly, beautiful.

Dignified too, with a grave clown's dignity,
A comic gravity and grace
That made us want to laugh at her
And yet remain respectful, loving and enthralled.
 Never was she morose, never beat, never
Intimated by the future, although if I
Was slow to fondle her she could pretend to pout.
 We had once handsome Pompey, a dalmatian dog,
A noble creature with a dignity of stance
And grace of movement no short-arsed corgi
Ever could approach – faithful also,
And aloof and stern, but he was often sad,
(Although he died before Hiroshima),
Melancholy, poor boy, and gloomy, deeply
Cast down before the vanity of our human wishes.
 But the little corgi bitch,
Her great uncalculating charm was perpetual,
Full-time, almost professional as a geisha girl's,
But far more innocent and exuberant,
More like a dashing Russian dancer's gaiety,
Leaping uninhibited in jet-black hat of astrakhan
And dishy long green coat and buckskin cossack
 boots.
But she was Welsh all right, Welsh of the Welsh,
Inbred Welsh, Welsh was her first language
Although she learnt some English too,
Words like *walks*, and *lead*, and *bones* –
And when she ran in rain her coat would smell,
Not of dog, but with the pungency of Teify flannel.
 Her ancient lineage, from the era of Hywel Dda,
Predated the Welsh Herberts' and Cecils', who, like
 her kin,
Shot up the social ladder, becoming courtiers
High in royal trust and favour, faithful darlings

Of Elizabeths; some cousins still remain unpaid
And poor auxiliaries of Dyfed cowboys, some are
    seen
About that tweedy world that tramps with shooting
    sticks
Across the pages of the posher magazines;
Some are yet short peasants predominant in palaces.
  When our memories,
Much that we recall, more we are haunted by,
Is shameful, is of loss and tears, suffering and death –
Blessings upon the miracle of Siani, comical, even
    absurd,
Bur handsome always, faithful, loving, droll,
Who by living, being, gave poor us delight,
Who, in a morning's sunlight, would run white-
    bibbed
Towards us, across the glittering lawn, grinning,
Her snow-white paws scattering sunlit
Dewdrops, scattering diamonds.

OGDEN NASH
Please Pass the Biscuit

I have a little dog,
Her name is Spangle.
And when she eats
I think she'll strangle.

She's darker then Hamlet,
Lighter than Porgy;
Her heart is gold,
Her odour, dorgy.

Her claws click-click
Across the floor,
Her nose is always
Against a door.

The squirrel flies
Her pursuing mouth;
Should he fly north;
She pursues him south.

Yet do not mock her
As she hunts;
Remember, she caught
A milkman once.

Like liquid gems
Her eyes burn clearly;
She's five years old,
And house-trained, nearly.

Her shame is deep
When she has erred;
She dreads the blow
Less than the word.

I marvel that such
Small ribs as these
Can cage such vast
Desire to please.

She's as much a part
Of the house as the mortgage;
Spangle, I wish you
A ripe old dortage.

❧

[94]

BEN GIMSON
Wild Thing

For Sorrel, a Golden Retriever
❧

Her ears prick.
    She quivers.
Something sparkles from her inner deep,
A glint behind her eyes.
Just a hint and she's away
To another world.

Scrub claws for water,
Clinging to rocky ranges,

Windswept, infertile.
Crusty black beetles
Crawl into their clefts.
The land lies, bloodless,
Flaking away like dead skin.
It's a battleground that
Smacks of death.
The sun scowls down
Upon mangled carcasses
 The losers
Of the savage arena.

– her limp body relaxes
In slumber before the fire.
The way we love her.
 How different
From the world we saw.
But as she twitches and
Snarls in her sleep,
A wild beast emerges,
Gleams from the deep.
 Not so far now
 From the barren
 Cruel land.

[95]

GWYNETH LEWIS
Good Dog!

All pets are part of one animal.
They look out at us from myriad eyes
hoping for food and a little love.
They themselves are unfailingly kind.
People who believe in reincarnation
feel the concern of departed relatives
shine from the heart of a new-born pup,
so confide in them, spoil them.
A well-placed 'Om' in a mongrel's ear
can save the soul of a dying dog.

Ours is theologian. This one knows
that sticks in life are more reliable than cats
and that balls are better. Everything thrown
is instantly precious, well worth running for.
The river he loves and tends to wear
it often. A Baptist, he immerses himself
with total abandon so his otter soul
is renewed in the feeder with the bags of crisps
and ribbons of algae.
He wears the medal of himself with joy.

His taste in art is for the Primitives.
He admires and collects all local sticks
and is a connoisseur of stones
which, being Staffordshire Bull, he eats.
He acquires the occasional traffic cone
for a hint of the abstract.

He finds that bushes all sprout balls,
mainly green and of the tennis kind,
a miraculous harvest which he daily reaps.

Something there is about a dog
draws conversation from frosty men
and available women. Trick for lonely boys and girls:
Get a dog. Walk him. For be it ugly or pure-bred,
a dog on a lead says: 'Here is a love
that makes its bargain with bad habits and smells,
the brute in a person, can accommodate needs
far other than its own, allows for beastliness.'

Some nights our lodger gets his favourite ball,
runs into the river and tramples the moon.

JAMES MERRILL
The Victor Dog

Bix to Buxtehude to Boulez,
The little white dog on the Victor label
Listens long and hard as he is able.
It's all in a day's work, whatever plays.

From judgment, it would seem, he has refrained.
He even listens earnestly to Bloch,
Then builds a church upon our acid rock.
He's man's – no – he's the Leiermann's best friend,

Or would be if hearing and listening were the same.
Does he hear? I fancy he rather smells
Those lemon-gold arpeggios in Ravel's
'Les jets d'eau du palais de ceux qui s'aiment.'

He ponders the Schumann Concerto's tall willow hit
By lightning, and stays put. When he surmises
Through one of Bach's eternal boxwood mazes
The oboe pungent as a bitch in heat,

Or when the calypso decants its raw bay rum
Or the moon in *Wozzeck* reddens ripe for murder,
He doesn't sneeze or howl; just listens harder.
Adamant needles bear down on him from

Whirling of outer space, too black, too near –
But he was taught as a puppy not to flinch,
Much less to imitate his bête noire Blanche
Who barked, fat foolish creature, at King Lear.

Still others fought in the road's filth over Jezebel,
Slavered on hearths of horned and pelted barons.
His forebears lacked, to say the least, forbearance.
Can nature change in him? Nothing's impossible.

The last chord fades. The night is cold and fine.
His master's voice rasps through the grooves' bare
    groves.
Obediently, in silence like the grave's
He sleeps there on the still-warm gramophone

Only to dream he is at the première of a Handel
Opera long thought lost – *Il Cane Minore*.
Its allegorical subject is his story!
A little dog revolving round a spindle

Gives rise to harmonies beyond belief,
A cast of stars . . . Is there in Victor's heart
No honey for the vanquished? Art is art.
The life it asks of us is a dog's life.

COLIN HURRY

Sam

Sir Samuel Batholiver Stilton Pug
Has enormous eyes and the quaintest mug,
A pushed-in nose that is far too small –
In fact it is hardly a nose at all –
Through which he breathes as well as he can
And snores when asleep like an old, old man.
A turned-down mouth is the fitting base
For a really surprisingly froglike face,
The ears are floppy and smooth to touch,
They're tiny too but they don't miss much.
A pattern of wrinkles round nose and eyes
Gives him that air of 'wild surmise'
Worn by stout Cortez and all his men
Once on a peak in Darien.
But Samuel Batholiver Stilton Pug
Would rather be wrapped in his Shetland rug
Than to be so venturesome as to go
Out on the conquest of Mexico.
For Samuel is not the adventuring kind,
Much preferring the things of the mind.
As I have said, his hearing's good
And you need not think you're misunderstood
If he doesn't obey at the first request:
He's just reflecting on what is best.
But let's continue describing Sam:
Champion blood in both sire and dam –
Merged in a most distinguished marriage –
Gave him an aristocratic carriage,

And though in front he's a froggy freak
He has a figure that's quite unique.
The ruff at his neck is a sign of breeding
But all these points are slowly leading
Up to his tail, his twice curled tail,
Tail before which all others pale,
Tail that coils in a grand disdain,
Tail that gives other tails a pain.
This he displays with a haughty shrug
Does Sir Samuel Batholiver Stilton Pug.
How was he named? You well may ask,
It wasn't a very easy task.
His Kennel name was the French Coq d'Or,
A name you could certainly not ignore.
It put us into a bit of a jam
Till somebody suddenly thought of SAM.

'Black-faced Sambo' was what they said
So Coq d'Or found himself Sam instead.
His knighthood came as a matter of course,
A step I am sure you will all endorse.
But why Batholiver? Stilton why?
This is the simple straight reply.
Sir Samuel is terribly fond of cheese,
Stilton for preference, if you please!
What is more, he prefers it fruity
With biscuits too. There, I've done my duty;
All's on record, the background's in,
Now let the story of Pugs begin,
Starting so long ago B.C.
That none can query its verity.
Now in the following thrilling pages
Read of the dog and the Chinese Sages.

☙

[98]

C. L. GRAVES
To Moses: A Spaniel

☙

Moses, old man, though unrenowned in story
   And hitherto unnoticed by the Press
You lead a life whose culminating glory
   Is when you earn your master's rare caress;
And though you do not shine in combats gory
   With other hounds, I do not love you less
For being what you are – a humble spaniel,
A dog that does not dare to be a Daniel.

You're not by any means a super-dog,
　　Though known to be an excellent retriever;
You cannot smoke a pipe or sip your grog
　　Like Consul, or build houses like a beaver;
You figure in no R.A. catalogue;
　　You were not thought of when the portrait fever
Lured the stout Peruvians to invest their boodle
In deadly likenesses of self and poodle.

You have the most ingratiating ways,
　　Although you cannot claim to be heroic
Like Gêlert, or to lead laborious days,
　　Or show the qualities of saint or Stoic;
In fact most of your instincts and your traits
　　Might be described as quite palæozoic;
And still, though all unversed in art and letters,
You are a model to your human betters.

Your fare is frugal; alcohol you bar;
　　Expensive liquors you have never guzzled;
Your comments on the Censor never jar,
　　Although you are allowed to go unmuzzled;
Your faith in man no cataclysm can mar;
　　By philosophic doubt you are not puzzled;
Nor do you find in hate a valid reason
For charging fallen Ministers with treason.

You know a lot about the O.T.C.;
　　And as your kennel flanks the office entry
You reinforce the bar of lock and key
　　By acting as an unofficial sentry,
Regarding passers-by, unless they be
　　Arrayed in khaki, as suspicious gentry,

But greeting with contortions of affection
The Major when he comes in your direction.

There seems a world of wisdom in your eyes,
    And yet your general conduct makes me wonder
Whether you can even dimly recognize
    The meaning of the cannons' muttered thunder,
Or read the menace of the moonless skies,
    Or guess how narrow are the seas that sunder
This land of peaceful water-meadows from
The shell-scarred wastes of Flanders and the Somme.

You are not stirred by passionate regret;
    You live and have your being in the present;
The greatest tragedy you've known as yet
    Is failure to retrieve a fallen pheasant;
You seldom need a visit from the vet.,
    The world to you is just as bright and pleasant
As when the Major first from Pangbourne brought
        you,
Where in the bulrush beds he saw and bought you.

Sometimes I wish, in hours of stress and strain,
    Your lucky limitations I could borrow,
And careless watch the seasons wax and wane,
    Unmoved by apprehensions for the morrow;
Then in a flash I see that life were vain
    Without the saving grace of human sorrow –
Which you can never know – the pain and pride
Caused us by those who greatly dared and died.

෧෨

THE REVD L. R. PHELPS
Oriel Bill

⁓

Thou, snub-nosed Satyr, in thy park
    Lulled by sweet strains of men
From 15 Oriel (bottom on the right),
    Snorest as loud as other dogs can bark.

Thou need'st not go to Schools, immortal dog!
    No fierce examiners thy toil can flout,
No books can e'er thy massive brain befog,
    Thou hold'st alike Vice-Chancellor and scout.
And yet oft-times thou, too, hast found thy way
    Into the dismal Schools, and thence thy nose,
Curled in disdain, away dost proudly turn.
    Thou, too, dost watch the play
At cricket or at football, and dost doze
    In tub or togger, leaping in astern.

⁓

REVD C. H. O. DANIEL
To Puffles

⁓

Oh Puffles, matted and hirsute,
Thou more than dog, thou less than brute;
Thou foe to cat, and rat, and bird,
Thou friend of man, thou beast absurd,

Thou dearest torment, genial curse,
That try'st my temper and my purse –
With what exulting headlong pace
Thou dost the mocking sparrow chase,
And then careering back again
Dost fill the street with yelping strain;
Or mud-bedraggled, leapest up
Upon my coat, exuberant pup!
While women fly and wheelmen curse,
And children crying, cling to nurse.
Thy ropy locks, thy dangling ears
Excite the host of prowling curs:
They, jealous of thy charms, combine
To wage on thee the war canine:
Thou fighting only when thou must
Dost roll the mongrels in the dust,
Then, clement as a dog of breed,
Leavest them peaceably to bleed.
And yet, the foe of all thy kind,
Thou hast a very gentle mind,
Though apt to fiercely bark like mad
At some innocuous Undergrad –
Who holds the Bursar's dog to be
The Bursar's demon worse than he.
Ah Puffles, dear detested friend,
Vices, and virtues, mingled blend.
I hate thee – yet I love thee more,
A four-legged angel, and a bore.

MARTIAL
To Issa

ᔆ

Issa is naughtier than Catallus's sparrow,
Issa is purer than the kiss of a dove,
Issa is more winsome than all girls,
Issa is dearer than jewels of India,
Issa is the pet bitch of Publius.
You think she is speaking if she whines;
She feels both sadness and joy.
She lies resting on his neck, and sleeps
So that no breathing is heard.
And when compelled by the requirements of her
   inside
She proves traitor to the coverlet by not one drop.
But with coaxing paw she rouses and warns
To be put down from the bed; and asks to be taken
   up.
Such is the modesty of the chaste little dog
That she is ignorant of Venus; nor can we find
A husband worthy of so tender a girl.
Lest death take her completely off,
Publius has expressed her in a painting,
In which you will see Issa so like
That not even she herself is so like herself.
Accordingly, compare Issa with the picture:
See which you will think is the real dog,
And which the painted one.

ᔆ

WILLIAM COWPER
On a Spaniel called Beau
Killing a Young Bird

A spaniel, Beau, that fares like you,
Well-fed, and at his ease,
Should wiser be, than to pursue
Each trifle that he sees.

But you have killed a tiny bird,
Which flew not till to-day,
Against my orders, whom you heard
Forbidding you the prey.

Nor did you kill that you might eat,
And ease a doggish pain;
For him, though chased with furious heat,
You left where he was slain.

Nor was he of the thievish sort,
Or one whom blood allures,
But innocent was all his sport,
Whom you have torn for yours.

My dog! What remedy remains,
Since, teach you all I can,
I see you, after all my pains,
So much resemble man!

WILLIAM COWPER
Beau's Reply

Sir! when I flew to seize the bird,
In spite of your command,
A louder voice than yours I heard,
And harder to withstand.

You cried 'Forbear!' – but in my breast
A mightier cried 'Proceed!'
'Twas Nature, Sir, whose strong behest
Impelled me to the deed.

Yet much as nature I respect,
I ventured once to break
(As you perhaps may recollect)
Her precept, for your sake;

And when your linnet, on a day,
Passing his prison door,
Had fluttered all his strength away,
And panting pressed the floor,

Well knowing him a sacred thing,
Not destined to my tooth,
I only kissed his ruffled wing,
And licked the feathers smooth.

Let my obedience then excuse
My disobedience now,
Nor some reproof yourself refuse
From your aggrieved Bow-wow!

If killing birds be such a crime,
(Which I can hardly see)
What think you, Sir, of killing Time
With verse addressed to me?

[104]

ALEXANDER POPE
Kew

Engraved on the collar of the dog presented to
Frederick, Prince of Wales

I am His Highness' dog at Kew
Pray tell me, sir, whose dog are you?

R.C. LEHMANN

Ave, Caesar!

Full in the splendour of this morning hour,
   With tramp of men and roll of muffled drums,
Lo what a pomp and pageantry of power,
   Borne to his grave, our Lord, King Edward comes!

In flashing gold and high magnificence,
   Lo, the proud cavalcade of comrade kings,
Met here to do the dead king reverence
   Its solemn tribute of affection brings.

Heralds and Pursuivants and Men-at-arms,
   Sultan, and Paladin and Potentate
Scarred Captains who have battled wars alarms
   And Courtiers glittering in their robes of state,

All in their blazoned ranks with eyes cast down,
   Slow pacing in their sorrow pass along
Where that which bore the sceptre and the crown
   Cleaves at their head the silence of the throng.

And in a space behind the passing bier,
   Looking and longing for his lord in vain,
A little playmate whom the King held dear
   Caesar, the terrier, tugs his silver chain!

Hail Caesar, lonely little Caesar, hail!
Little for you the gathered kings avail.
Little you reck, as meekly past you go,
Of that solemnity of formal woe.

In the strange silence, lo, you prick your ear
For one loved voice and that you shall not hear.
So when the monarchs with their bright array
Of gold and steel and stars have passed away,
When, to their wonted use restored again,
All things go duly in their ordered train,
You shall appeal at each excluding door,
Search through the rooms and every haunt explore;
From lawn to lawn, from path to path pursue
The well-loved form that still escapes your view.
At every tree some happy memories rise
To stir your tail and animate your eyes,
And at each turn, with gathering strength endued,
Hope, still frustrated, still must be renewed.
How shall you rest from your appointed task,
Till chance restore the happiness you ask,
Take from your heart the burden, ease the pain,
And grant you to your master's side again,
Proud and content if but you could beguile
His voice to flatter and his face to smile?

Caesar, the kindly days may bring relief;
Swiftly they pass and dull the edge of grief.
You too, resigned at last, may school your mind
To miss the comrade whom you cannot find,
Never forgetting, but as one who feels
The world has secrets which no skill reveals.
Henceforth, whate'er the ruthless fates may give
You shall be loved and cherished while you live
Reft of your master, little dog forlorn,
To one dear mistress you shall now be sworn,
And in her queenly service you shall dwell,
At rest with one who loved your master well.
And she, that gentle lady shall control

The faithful kingdom of a true dog's soul,
And for the past's dear sake shall still defend
Caesar, the dead King's humble little friend.

[106]

SIR JOHN SQUIRE
To a Bull-dog

(W. H. S., Capt. (Acting Major),
R. F. A.; killed April 12th, 1917)

We sha'n't see Willy any more, Mamie,
    He won't be coming any more:
He came back once and again and again,
    But he won't get leave any more.

We looked from the window and there was his cab,
    And we ran downstairs like a streak,
And he said, 'Hullo, you bad dog,' and you crouched
        to the floor,
    Paralysed to hear him speak,

And then let fly at his face and his chest
    Till I had to hold you down,
While he took off his cap and his gloves and his coat,
    And his bag and his thonged Sam Browne.

We went upstairs to the studio,
    The three of us, just as of old,
And you lay down and I sat and talked to him
    As round the room he strolled.

Here in the room where, years ago
    Before the old life stopped,
He worked all day with his slippers and his pipe,
    He would pick up the threads he'd dropped,

Fondling all the drawings he had left behind,
    Glad to find them all still the same,
And opening the cupboards to look at his belongings
    . . . Every time he came.

But now I know what a dog doesn't know,
    Though you'll thrust your head on my knee,
And try to draw me from the absent-mindedness
    That you find so dull in me.

And all your life you will never know
    What I wouldn't tell you even if I could,
That the last time we waved him away
    Willy went for good.

But sometimes as you lie on the hearthrug
    Sleeping in the warmth of the stove,
Even through your muddled old canine brain
    Shapes from the past may rove.

You'll scarcely remember, even in a dream,
    How we brought home a silly little pup,
With a big square head and little crooked legs
    That could scarcely bear him up,

But your tail will tap at the memory
    Of a man whose friend you were,
Who was always kind though he called you a naughty dog
    When he found you on his chair;

Who'd make you face a reproving finger
    And solemnly lecture you
Till your head hung downwards and you looked very
      sheepish!
    And you'll dream of your triumphs too.

Of summer evening chases in the garden
    When you dodged us all about with a bone:
We were three boys, and you were the cleverest,
    But now we're two alone.

When summer comes again,
    And the long sunsets fade,
We shall have to go on playing the feeble game for
      two
    That since the war we've played.

And though you run expectant as you always do
    To the uniforms we meet,
You'll never find Willy among all the soldiers
    In even the longest street,

Nor in any crowd; yet, strange and bitter thought,
    Even now were the old words said,
If I tried the old trick and said, 'Where's Willy?'
    You would quiver and lift your head,

And your brown eyes would look to ask if I were
      serious,
    And wait for the word to spring.
Sleep undisturbed: I shan't say *that* again,
    You innocent old thing.

I must sit, not speaking, on the sofa,
    While you lie asleep on the floor;

For he's suffered a thing that dogs couldn't dream of,
  And he won't be coming here any more.

[107]

ANONYMOUS
Greyfriars Bobby

I hear they say 'tis very lang
  That years hae come and gane,
Sin' first they put my maister here,
  An' grat an' left him lane.
I could na, an' I did na gang,
  For a' they vexed me sair,
An' said sae bauld that they nor I
  Should ever see him mair.

I ken he's near me a' the while,
  An' I will see him yet;
For a' my life he tended me,
  An' noo he'll not forget.

Some blithsome day I'll hear his step;
  There'll be nae kindred near;
For a' they grat, they gaed awa', –
  But he shall find *me* here.

Is time sae lang? – I dinna mind;
  Is't cauld? – I canna feel;
He's near me, and he'll come to me,
  And sae 'tis very weel.
I thank ye a' that are sae kind,
  As feed an' mak me braw;
Ye're unco gude, but ye're no *him* –
  Ye'll no wile me awa.

I'll bide an' hope! – Do ye the same;
  For ance I heard that ye
Had aye a Master that ye loo'd,
  An' yet ye might na' see;
A Master, too, that car'd for ye,
  (O, sure ye winna flee!)
That's wearying to see ye noo –
  Ye'll no be waur than me?'

SIR WALTER SCOTT

FROM

Marmion

෧෨

Decided drifts the flaky snow,
And forth the hardy swain must go.
Long with dejected look and whine,
To leave the hearth his dogs repine:
Whistling and cheering them to aid
Around his back he wreathes his plaid:
His flock he gathers, and he guides,
To open downs and mountain-sides,
Where fiercest though the tempest blow,
Least deeply lies the drift below.

If fails his heart, if his limbs fail,
Benumbing death is in the gale:
His paths, his landmarks all unknown,
Close to the hut no more his own,
Close to the aid he sought in vain,
The morn may find the stiffened swain:
The widow sees, at dawning pale
His orphans raise their feeble wail:
And, close beside him in the snow,
Poor Yarrow, partner of their woe,
Crouches upon his master's breast,
And licks his cheek to break his rest.

෧෨

SIR WALTER SCOTT
Helvellyn

I climb'd the dark brow of the mighty Helvellyn,
  Lakes and mountains beneath me gleam'd misty and
     wide;
All was still, save by fits, when the eagle was yelling,
  And starting around me the echoes replied.
On the right, Striden-edge round the Red-tarn was
     bending,
And Catchedicam its left verge was defending,
One huge nameless rock in the front was ascending,
  Where I mark'd the sad spot where the wand'rer
     had died.

Dark green was that spot 'mid the brown mountain-
     heather,
  Where the Pilgrim of Nature lay stretch'd in decay,
Like the corpse of an outcast abandon'd to weather,
  Till the mountain winds wasted the tenantless clay.
Nor yet quite deserted, though lonely extended,
For, faithful in death, his mute favourite attended,
The much-loved remains of her master defended,
  And chased the hill-fox and the raven away.

How long didst thou think that his silence was
     slumber?
  When the wind waved his garment, how oft didst
     thou start?
How many long days and long weeks didst thou
     number,

Ere he faded before thee, the friend of thy heart?
And, oh, was it meet, that – no requiem read o'er
      him –
No mother to weep, and no friend to deplore him,
And thou, little guardian, alone stretch'd before him –
  Unhonour'd the Pilgrim from life should depart?

When a Prince to the fate of the Peasant has yielded,
  The tapestry waves dark round the dim-lighted hall;
With scutcheons of silver the coffin is shielded,
  And pages stand mute by the canopied pall:
Through the courts, at deep midnight, the torches are
      gleaming;
In the proudly-arch'd chapel the banners are beaming,
Far adown the long aisle sacred music is streaming,
  Lamenting a Chief of the people should fall.

But meeter for thee, gentle lover of Nature,
  To lay down thy head like the meek mountain lamb,
When, wilder'd, he drops from some cliff huge in
      stature,
  And draws his last sob by the side of his dam.
And more stately thy couch by this desert lake lying,
Thy obsequies sung by the grey plover flying,
With one faithful friend but to witness thy dying,
  In the arms of Helvellyn and Catchedicam.

❧

[110]

BRENDA CHAMBERLAIN
*To Dafydd Coed Mourning his
Mountain-broken Dog*

❧

Tears that you spill, clown David, crouched by rock
Have changed to nightmare quartzite, chips of
      granite.
The valley chokes with grief-stones wept from eyes
New-taught that death-scythes flash in the riven block
To reap warm entrails for a raven-harvest.
Withdrawn in stone-shot gully of the barren ground;
You mourn, baffled by crevice and goat height
Proving tricksy as dog-fox run to earth in the scree,
For one who lies in company of beetle-shard and
      sheep,
For him whose loose dropped brain and lungs hang
      coldly

Trembling from the flowered ledge down ice plant
    ways to silence.
The tears you shed are stone. So leave the dead to
    stand as monument.
Be shepherd friend again, clown grinning under wet
    eyes,
Stopping your ears to sound the valley breeds:
A corpse-man's cry for succour, a dead dog's howl.

[111]

HENRY LAWSON
The Cattle-dog's Death

The plains lay bare on the homeward route,
And the march was heavy on man and brute;
For the Spirit of Drouth was on all the land,
And the white heat danced on the glowing sand.

The best of our cattle-dogs lagged at last;
His strength gave out ere the plains were passed;
And our hearts were sad as he crept and laid
His languid limbs in the nearest shade.

He saved our lives in the years gone by,
When no one dreamed of the danger nigh,
And treacherous blacks in the darkness crept
On the silent camp where the white men slept.

'Rover is dying,' a stockman said,
As he knelt and lifted the shaggy head;
' 'Tis a long day's march ere the run be near,
And he's going fast; shall we leave him here?'

But the super cried, 'There's an answer there!'
As he raised a tuft of the dog's grey hair;
And, strangely vivid, each man descried
The old spear-mark on the shaggy hide.

We laid a bluey and coat across
A camp-pack strapped on the lightest horse,
Then raised the dog to his deathbed high,
And brought him far 'neath the burning sky.

At the kindly touch of the stockmen rude
His eyes grew human with gratitude;
And though we were parched, when his eyes grew
    dim
The last of our water was given to him.

The super's daughter we knew would chide
If we left the dog in the desert wide;
So we carried him home o'er the burning sand
For a parting stroke from her small white hand.

But long ere the station was seen ahead,
His pain was o'er, for Rover was dead;
And the folks all knew by our looks of gloom
'Twas a comrade's corpse that we carried home.

[112]

ANONYMOUS

FROM

The Road Dog

Up to the front of 'em, back to the rear
Nipping the stocking and tweaking the ear,
Staying the quick of 'em, lifting the sick of 'em,
Over 'em, under 'em, into the thick of 'em,
Right of 'em, left of 'em, hazing 'em, holding 'em,
Somehow or other he's ended by folding 'em.

VIRGIL

FROM

Georgics

TRANSLATED BY
John Dryden

Nor, last, forget thy faithful dogs; but feed
With fattening whey the mastiff's generous breed,
And Spartan race, who, for the fold's relief,
Will persecute with cries the nightly thief,
Repulse the prowling wolf, and hold at bay
The mountain robbers rushing to the prey.

[114]

W. R. SPENCER

FROM

*Beth Gelert, or the Grave
of the Greyhound*

The spearmen heard the bugle sound,
And cheerly smiled the morn;
And many a brach, and many a hound,
Obeyed Llewelyn's horn.

And still he blew a louder blast,
And gave a lustier cheer;
'Come Gelert, Come, wert never last
Llewelyn's horn to hear.'

'Oh, where does faithful Gelert roam,
The flower of all his race;
So true, so brave, a lamb at home,
A lion in the chase?'

'Twas only at Llewelyn's board
The faithful Gelert fed;
He watched, he served, he cheered his lord,
And sentinelled his bed.

In sooth he was a peerless hound,
The gift of royal John;
But, now no Gelert could be found,
And all the chase rode on.

And now, as o'er the rocks and dells
The gallant chidings rise,
All Snowdon's craggy chaos yells
The many mingled cries!

That day Llewelyn little loved
The chase of hart and hare;
And scant and small the booty proved,
For Gelert was not there.

Unpleased Llewelyn homeward hied,
When near the portal-seat,
His truant Gelert he espied
Bounding his lord to greet.

But when he gained his castle-door
Aghast the chieftain stood;
The hound all o'er was smeared with gore,
His lips, his fangs, ran blood.

Llewelyn gazed with fierce surprise;
Unused such looks to meet,
His favourite checked his joyful guise,
And crouched, and licked his feet.

Onward, in haste, Llewelyn passed,
And on went Gelert too;
And still, where'er his eyes he cast,
Fresh blood-gouts shocked his view.

O'erturned his infant's bed he found,
With blood-stained covert rent;
And all around the walls and ground
With recent blood besprent.

He called his child – no voice replied –
He searched with terror wild;
Blood, blood, he found on every side,
But nowhere found his child.

'Hell-hound! my child's by thee devoured,'
The frantic father cried;
And to the hilt his vengeful sword
He plunged in Gelert's side.

His suppliant looks, as prone he fell,
No pity could impart;
But still his Gelert's dying yell
Passed heavy o'er his heart.

Aroused by Gelert's dying yell
Some slumberer wakened nigh: –
What words the parent's joy could tell
To hear his infant's cry!

Concealed beneath a tumbled heap
His hurried search had missed,
All glowing from his rosy sleep,
The cherub boy he kissed.

Nor scathe had he, nor harm, nor dread,
But, the same couch beneath,
Lay, a gaunt wolf, all torn and dead,
Tremendous still in death.

Ah! what was then Llewelyn's pain!
For now the truth was clear;
His gallant hound the wolf had slain
To save Llewelyn's heir.

Vain, vain, was all Llewelyn's woe:
'Best of thy kind, adieu!
The frantic blow which laid thee low
This heart shall ever rue.'

And now a gallant tomb they raise,
With costly sculpture decked;
And marbles storied with his praise,
Poor Gelert's bones protect.

There never could the spearmen pass,
Or forester, unmoved;
There, oft the tear-besprinkled grass
Llewelyn's sorrow proved.

And there he hung his horn and spear,
And there, as evening fell,
In fancy's ear he oft would hear
Poor Gelert's dying yell.

And, till great Snowdon's rocks grow old,
And cease the storm to brave,
The consecrated spot shall hold
The name of 'Gelert's Grave.'

[115]

THE BIBLE

FROM

2 Kings

Chapter 8 Verse 13

Is thy servant a dog that he should do this
great thing?

RICHARD MURPHY
The Wolfhound

A wolfhound sits under a wild ash
Licking the wound in a dead ensign's neck.

When guns cool at night with bugles in fog
She points over the young face.

All her life a boy's pet.
Prisoners are sabred and the dead are stripped.

Her ear pricks like a crimson leaf on snow,
The horse-carts creak away.

Vermin by moonlight pick
The tongues and sockets of six thousand skulls.

She pines for his horn to blow
To bay in triumph down the track of wolves.

Her forelegs stand like pillars through a siege,
His Toledo sword corrodes.

Nights she lopes to the scrub
And trails back at dawn to guard a skeleton.

Wind shears the berries from the rowan tree,
The wild geese have flown.

She lifts her head to cry
As a woman keens in a famine for her son.

A redcoat, stalking, cocks
His flintlock when he hears the wolfhound growl.

Her fur bristles with fear at the new smell,
Snow has betrayed her lair.

'I'll sell you for a packhorse,
You antiquated bigoted papistical bitch!'

She springs: in self-defence he fires his gun.
People remember this.

By turf embers she gives tongue
When the choirs are silenced in wood and stone.

[117]

SUSAN HAMLYN
Attila Takes a Hand

We drive through the gateway,
Get out of the car
And see to our horror
The door is ajar.

'My God! We've been burgled!
It's happened again!
Perhaps they're still in there?
Bad boys? Or tough men?

'But where is Attila?
Where *is* that beast?
We thought the Alsatian
Would scare them at least.

'Oh, here is the hero!
And wagging his tail!
Why didn't you give them
The CDs as well?

'Get back to the kitchen!
Guard dog indeed!
No one so cowardly
Should wear collar and lead!'

Attila slinks out
But then, strangely, lingers
And sniffs by his forepaw
Two fresh human fingers.

ELIZABETH BARRETT BROWNING
Flush

But of *Thee* it shall be said,
This dog watched beside a bed
   Day and night unweary,
Watched within a curtained room
Where no sunbeam brake the gloom
   Round the sick and dreary.

Roses, gathered for a vase,
In that chamber died apace,
   Beam and breeze resigning;
This dog only, waited on,
Knowing that when light is gone
   Love remains for shining.

T. HODGKINSON
The Flatterer

(It is suggested that dogs should be trained to find balls
lost on the golf links.)

For tricks that are smart and for ways that are
   winning,
My Fido you've long had a goodly repute,
And after your recent auspicious beginning

I think as a golf-hound you're certain to suit;
It isn't so much that you proved yourself clever
    In finding the balls that I chanced to deflect
As the comforting way that your ardent endeavour
        Was fruitful in moral effect.

I hadn't proceeded as far as the second
    Before a by no means unusual slice
Produced a result which I honestly reckoned
    Excused me from murmuring 'Bother it' (twice);
'Twas not with much hope that I bade you to seek it,
    But I waited to see your response to my call
Ere sadly I further diminished my wee kit
        And dropped an expensive new ball.

Yet I couldn't but joy in your manner of working,
    When, quitting my loss's immediate scene,
As though you'd deduced where the pillule was
        lurking
    You tactfully made for the proximate green;
I couldn't but joy at the faith you attested,
    Though ground for such faith I had given you none,
When you nosed in the hole in a way that suggested
        You thought I had done it in one.

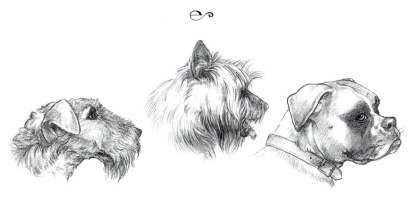

WILLIAM COWPER
The Dog and the Water-lily
No Fable

The noon was shady, and soft airs
 Swept Ouse's silent tide,
When, 'scaped from literary cares,
 I wandered on his side.

My spaniel, prettiest of his race,
 And high in pedigree,
(Two nymphs, adorned with every grace,
 That spaniel found for me)

Now wantoned, lost in flags and reeds,
 Now starting into sight
Pursued the swallow o'er the meads
 With scarce a slower flight.

It was the time when Ouse displayed
 His lilies newly blown;
Their beauties I intent surveyed;
 And one I wished my own.

With cane extended far I sought
 To steer it close to land;
But still the prize, though nearly caught,
 Escaped my eager hand.

Beau marked my unsuccessful pains
 With fixed considerate face,
And puzzling sat his puppy brains
 To comprehend the case.

But with a chirrup clear and strong
  Dispersing all his dream,
I thence withdrew, and followed long
  The windings of the stream.

My ramble finished, I returned;
  Beau trotting far before,
The floating wreath again discerned,
  And plunging left the shore.

I saw him with that lily cropped
  Impatient swim to meet
My quick approach, and soon he dropped
  The treasure at my feet.

Charmed with the sight, 'The world,' I cried,
  'Shall hear of this thy deed:
My dog shall mortify the pride
  Of man's superior breed.'

But, chief, myself I will enjoin,
  Awake at duty's call,
To show a love as prompt as thine
  To Him who gives me all.

MAUREEN MELVIN
Apache – He Say . . .

I know that God created man
And all that sort of thing.
He made the sun, the moon, the stars
And taught the birds to sing.

I know He loves the underdog
And those who've gone astray.
He even spells His Name like ours
But round the other way!

Apache Indians put their trust
In different kinds of god.
Some views they hold are wonderful
And some are rather odd.

But one thing sets my heart aglow,
One thing and one thing only –
The thought that God created Man
So Dog would not be lonely.

[122]

ALEXANDER POPE
FROM
Essay on Man

To Be, contents his natural desire,
He asks no Angel's wing, nor Seraph's fire:
But thinks, admitted to that equal sky,
His faithful dog shall bear him company.

[123]

ANONYMOUS
Pansy (a Pekinese)

Died Sunday, June 6th 1937, aged 5 ½ years,
Longleat, Wiltshire

Brave little huntress ever true
Engraved upon my heart are you
No one can fill your special place
My Pansy with a sooty face

Darling I hope they give to you
Budgerigars to hunt of blue
Rabbits of black and white in cages
And rats to shake throughout the ages

And when I stand alone and grey
Outside the forest, Lord I pray
That I may hear her little bark
To lead me through the unknown dark.

[124]

LOUISE IMOGEN GUINEY
To a Dog's Memory

The gusty morns are here,
When all the reeds ride low with level spear;
And on such nights as lured us far of yore,
Down rocky alleys yet, and through the pine,
The Hound-star and the pagan Hunter shine;
But I and thou, ah, field-fellow of mine,
Together roam no more.

Soft showers go laden now
With odors of the sappy orchard-bough,
And brooks begin to brawl along the march;
The late frost steams from hollow sedges high;
The finch is come, the flame-blue dragon-fly,
The cowslip's common gold that children spy,
The plume upon the larch.

There is a music fills
The oaks of Belmont and the Wayland hills
Southward to Dewing's little bubbly stream,
The heavenly weather's call! O, who alive
Hastes not to start, delays not to arrive,
Having free feet that never felt a gyve
Weigh, even in a dream?

But thou, instead, hast found
The sunless April uplands underground
And still, wherever thou art, I must be.
My beautiful! arise in might and mirth,
For we were tameless travellers from our birth;
Arise against thy narrow door of earth,
And keep the watch for me.

PATRICK CHALMERS
Crib Mourned

Crib, on your grave beneath the chestnut boughs,
Today no fragrance falls nor summer air,
Only a master's love who laid you there
Perchance may warm the earth 'neath which you
    drowse
In dreams from which no dinner gong may rouse,
Unwakeable, though close the rat may dare,
Deaf, though the rabbit thumps in playful scare,
Silent, though twenty tabbies pay their vows.
And yet, mayhap, some night when shadows pass,
And from the fir the brown owl hoots on high,
That should one whistle 'neath a favouring star
Your small white shade shall patter o'er the grass,
Questing for him you loved o' days gone by,
Ere Death, the Dog-Thief, carried you afar!

GODFREY ELTON
Lugete Veneres

Now that my little dog is dead
The endless winds blow over his head,
And he is very far, alone,
From the men and towns that were his own.

In Berkshire woods he should have lain,
In pine-woods whispering with the rain,
Or by his dear pool, clear and deep,
In Berkshire slept his endless sleep.

So might I stand, and think again,
Of our long rambles in the rain,
Or call for him to come to me
Across the woods by Eversley.

Now that my little dog is dead
There are three poplars at his head,
And he is lying very still
Under a meadow on a hill.

I can see him lying – three foot deep –
He is sleeping now as he used to sleep.
He is lying now as he used to lie,
With his four paws stretched so patiently.

Waiting for some clear, summer dawning,
And for my whistle in the morning.
But the man he loved is far away,
And his night ends not in any day.

The endless winds above him sing,
And pattering rain at evening;
He is dwindling to a skeleton,
My dainty one, my lovely one.

Sleep well, Mick, by your poplar trees,
Sleep on, fear nothing, be at ease;
Somewhere, somehow we'll meet again,
And go long rambles in the rain.

ℰↄ

FRANCIS JAMMES
Blessed Being

Now you are dead, my faithful dog, my humble
    friend.
Dead of the death that like a wasp you fled,
Where under the table you would hide. Your head
Was turned to me in the brief and bitter end.

O mate of man! Blest being! You that shared
Your master's hunger and his meals as well! . . .
You that in days of old, in pilgrimage fared
With young Tobias and the angel Raphael. . . .

Servant that loved me with a love intense,
As saints love God, my great exemplar be! . . .
The mystery of your deep intelligence
Dwells in a guiltless, glad eternity.

Dear Lord! If you should grant me by Your grace
To see You face to face in Heaven, O then
Grant that a poor dog look into the face
Of him who was his god here among men! . . .

WINIFRED M. LETTS
Tim an Irish Terrier

It's wonderful dogs they're breeding now;
Small as a flea or large as a cow;
But my old lad Tim he'll never be bet
By any dog that ever he met.
'Come on', says he, 'For I'm not kilt yet.'

No matter the size of the dog he'll meet,
Tim trails his coat the length of the street.
D'ye mind his scars and his ragged ear,
The like of a Dublin Fusilier?
He's a massacree dog that knows no fear.

But he'd stick to me till his latest breath;
An' he'd go with me to the gates of death.
He'd wait for a thousand years maybe;
Scratching the door and whining for me
If myself were inside in Purgatory.

So I laugh when I hear them make it plain
That dogs and men never meet again.
For all their talk who'd listen to them
With the soul in the shining eyes of him?
Would God be wasting a dog like Tim?

[129]

R. E. VERNEDE

To an English Sheep-dog

Old Dog, what times we had, you, she and I,
Since first you came and with your trustful air
Blundered into her lap – a valiant, shy,
    Small tub-shaped woolly bear.

What lovely days we had; how fast they flew
In hill-side ramblings, gallopings by the sea:
You grew too large for laps but never grew
    Too large for loyalty.

We have known friends who living passed away –
Your faith no man could turn, no passion kill;
Even when Death called, you would scarce obey
    Until you knew our will.

Out in the fields I bore you in my arms,
Dear Thick-coat, on your grave the grasses spring;
But He that sees no sparrow meets with harms
        Hath your soul's shepherding.

And will that King who knows all hearts and ways
Kennel you where the winds blow long and fair
That you who ever loathed the warm still days
        May snuff an upland air?

And will He let you scamper o'er the meads
Where His hills close their everlasting ranks,
And show you pools that mirror gray-green reeds
        To cool your heaving flanks?

And will He feed you with good things at even,
Bringing the bowl with His own hands maybe?
And will you, hunting in your dreams in Heaven,
        Dream that you hunt with me?

Yes, you will not forget; and when we come,
What time or by what gate we may not tell,
Hastening to meet our friend that men call dumb
        Across the ditch of Hell,

You'll hear, you first of all, oh, strong and fleet,
How you will dash, an arrow to the mark!
Lord, but there'll be deaf angels when we meet –
        And you leap up and bark!

⁓ 183 ⁓

R. C. LEHMANN
To Rufus, a Spaniel

Rufus! there are who hesitate to own
Merits, they say, your master sees alone.
They judge you stupid, for you show no bent
To any poodle-dog accomplishment.

. . .

Well, let them rail. If since your life began,
Beyond the customary lot of man
Staunchness was yours; if of your faithful heart
Malice and scorn could never claim a part;
If in your master, loving while you live,
You own no fault or own it to forgive;
If, as you lay your head upon his knee,
Your deep-drawn sighs proclaim your sympathy;
If faith and friendship, growing with your age,
Speak through your eyes and all his love engage;
If by that master's wish your life you rule –
If this be folly, *Rufus*, you're a fool.
Old dog, content you; *Rufus*, have no fear:
While life is yours and mine your place is here.
And when the day shall come, as come it must,
When *Rufus* goes to mingle with the dust
(If Fate ordains that you shall pass before
To the abhorred and sunless Stygian shore),
I think old Charon, punting through the dark,
Will hear a sudden friendly little bark;
And on the shore he'll mark without a frown
A flap-eared doggie, bandy-legged and brown.

He'll take you in: since watermen are kind,
He'd scorn to leave my little dog behind.
He'll ask no obol, but instal you there
On Styx's further bank without a fare.
There shall you sniff his cargoes as they come,
And droop your head, and turn, and still be dumb –
Till one fine day, half joyful, half in fear,
You run and prick a recognising ear,
And last, oh, rapture! leaping to his hand,
Salute your master as he steps to land.

☙

[131]

ROBERT SERVICE
The Outlaw

☙

A wild and woeful race he ran
Of lust and sin by land and sea;
Until, abhorred of God and man,
They swung him from the gallows-tree.
And then he climbed the Starry Stair,
And dumb and naked and alone,
With head unbowed and brazen glare,
He stood before the Judgment Throne.

The Keeper of the Records spoke:
'This man, O Lord, has mocked Thy Name.
The weak have wept beneath his yoke,
The strong have fled before his flame.

The blood of babes is on his sword;
His life is evil to the brim:
Look down, decree his doom, O Lord!
Lo! there is none will speak for him.'

The golden trumpets blew a blast
That echoed in the crypts of Hell,
For there was Judgment to be passed,
And lips were hushed and silence fell.
The man was mute; he made no stir
Erect before the Judgment Seat . . .
When all at once a mongrel cur
Crept out and cowered and licked his feet.

It licked his feet with whining cry.
Come Heav'n, come Hell, what did it care?
It leapt, it tried to catch his eye;
Its master, yea, its God was there.
Then, as a thrill of wonder sped
Through throngs of shining seraphim,
The Judge of All looked down and said:
'Lo! here is *One* who pleads for him.'

RUDYARD KIPLING
Dinah in Heaven

She did not know that she was dead,
  But, when the pang was o'er,
Sat down to wait her Master's tread
  Upon the Golden Floor.

With ears full-cock and anxious eyes,
  Impatiently resigned;
But ignorant that Paradise
  Did not admit her kind.

Persons with Haloes, Harps, and Wings
  Assembled and reproved;
Or talked to her of Heavenly things,
  But Dinah never moved.

There was one step along the Stair
  That led to Heaven's Gate;
And, till she heard it, her affair
  Was – she explained – to wait.

And she explained with flattened ear,
  Bared lip and milky tooth –
Storming against Ithuriel's Spear
  That only proved her truth!

Sudden – far down the Bridge of Ghosts
  That anxious spirits clomb –
She caught that step in all the hosts,
  And knew that he had come.

She left them wondering what to do,
　But not a doubt had she.
Swifter than her own squeal she flew
　Across the Glassy sea;

Flushing the Cherubs everywhere,
　And skidding as she ran,
She refuged under Peter's Chair
　And waited for her man.

. . .

There spoke a Spirit out of the press
　'Said: – 'Have you any here
That saved a fool from drunkenness,
　And a coward from his fear?

'That turned a soul from dark to day
　When other help was vain;
That snatched it from wan hope and made
　A cur a man again?'

'Enter and look,' said Peter then,
　And set The Gate ajar.
'If I know aught of women and men
　I trow she is not far.'

'Neither by virtue, speech nor art
　Nor hope of grace to win;
But godless innocence of heart
　That never heard of sin:

'Neither by beauty nor belief
　Nor white example shown.
Something a wanton – more a thief –
　But – most of all – mine own.'

'Enter and look,' said Peter then,
  'And send you well to speed;
But, for all that I know of women and men
  Your riddle is hard to read.'

Then flew Dinah from under the Chair,
  Into his arms she flew –
And licked his face from chin to hair
  And Peter passed them through!

ℯ

[133]

JOE WALKER
The Quest
ℯ

Across the golden floor he strayed,
Unkempt and tired, but undismayed,
And in and out and up and down
He searched, and sniffed each saintly gown
Whilst scandalized arch-angels shooed,
And seraphs ceased their song and booed.
'I want my friend – my master dear!'
'Hence, mangy cur – he is not here;
He was a sinner. . . .'
                    'That may be,
But he was always good to me.
You need not fear I'd wish to stay
In Heaven without my Man.   Good day.'
He left in haste the Blest Abode,
And, joyous, took the Lower Road.

ℯ

SEAMUS HEANEY

A Dog *was* Crying Tonight in Wicklow Also

in memory of Donatus Nwoga

When human beings found out about death
They sent the dog to Chukwu with a message:
They wanted to be let back to the house of life.
They didn't want to end up lost forever
Like burnt wood disappearing into smoke
Or ashes that get blown away to nothing.
Instead, they saw their souls in a flock at twilight
Cawing and headed back for the same old roosts
And the same bright airs and wing-stretching each
    morning.
Death would be like a night spent in the wood:
At first light they'd be back in the house of life.
(The dog was meant to tell all this to Chukwu).

But death and human beings took second place
When he trotted off the path and started barking
At another dog in broad daylight just barking
Back at him from the far bank of a river.

And that is how the toad reached Chukwu first,
The toad who'd overheard in the beginning
What the dog was meant to tell. 'Human beings,'
    he said
(And here the toad was trusted absolutely),
'Human beings want death to last forever.'

Then Chukwu saw the people's souls in birds
Coming towards him like black spots off the sunset
To a place where there would be neither roosts nor
    trees
Nor any way back to the house of life.
And his mind reddened and darkened all at once
And nothing that the dog would tell him later
Could change that vision. Great chiefs and great
    loves
In obliterated light, the toad in mud,
The dog crying out all night behind the corpse
    house.

[135]

JOE WALKER

The Dog in the Manger

Was there a dog – and did he raise his head
As to the stable by the great star led,
Drew near the Wise Men in their proud array
To pay glad homage on that Christmas Day?

'*Who goes there? Strangers!*' Then inside he'd trot
And stand on guard beside the lowly cot,
Till, reassured, he'd strive to make amends,
'*I didn't know, you see, that you were friends.*'
Then, as they knelt and proffered gifts most rare,
I fancy him, delighted, standing there,
Till, reverence paid, they pass into the night
Watched by him keenly till they fade from sight,
Then back he creeps into that stable dim.

'*A dog?*' Who knows? I like to picture him.

[136]

PHILIP GELL

Landscape: Dog Looking at a Bird

My dog checks, is poised in frozen motion
Seeing a bird – he knows it is of his same creation

The cat leaps the gate, pauses on the rail
In one pure wave of motion from head to tail

The cows gaze from eyes that are candid and clear
They are innocent of desire, have no wish to interfere

The rats rustle in the hedgerow and creep in the barn
Proud, wise, and ambitious, everything is their
    concern

Too clever by half, the bipedal animals drive
Their iron machines on the high road – tarred,
    fenced, no longer alive

These multiply too fast, consume their own kind
Their brother animals are free, they are confined

Let them recollect that dogs, cats, cows and rats are
    of the same creation
Citizens of the same town and county, members of the
    same nation
Let them practise loving the rats in the barn, in order
To love the better the people in the next house
    or on the other side of the national border.

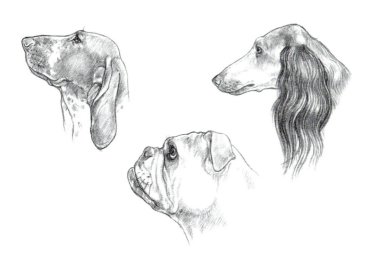

WILLIAM SHAKESPEARE
FROM
Macbeth
Act III Scene i

First murderer We are men, my liege.
Macbeth Ay, in the catalogue ye go for men,
As hounds, and greyhounds, mongrels, spaniels, curs,
Shoughes, water-rugs, and demi-wolves, are 'clept
All by the name of dogs; the valued file
Distinguishes the swift, the slow, the subtle,
The house-keeper, the hunter, every one
According to the gift which bounteous Nature
Hath in him closed – whereby he does receive
Particular addition from the bill
That writes them all alike; – and so of men.

FIONA OWEN
The Dog Shoot

Sunday morning and we awoke to the pop-pop of
    guns.
Across the stretch of sand, near the Bedouin village,
a Sharjah soldier had a shot dog by a back leg,
one of the pye dogs that we fed.

There was a whole heap of them, chucked
into an old oil drum on the back of a lorry.
Most were not quite dead. Wet noses
stuck out all uneven, paws paddling the air
as if in safe dreams. The whole drum heaved
like a can of caught worms.

We scampered about the compound
tripping in the sand, fetching dogs in
until the house was packed out with those saved.
Then we pounded after the truck, waving our arms.
My mother fell on the subca track and split
her seventies tight pink pants from seam to seam.

SPIKE MILLIGAN
The Dog Lovers

So they bought you
And kept you in a
Very good home
Central heating
TV
A deep freeze
A *very* good home –
No one to take you
For that lovely long run –
But otherwise
'A *very* good home'.
They fed you Pal and Chum
But not that lovely long run,
Until, mad with energy and boredom
You escaped – and ran and ran and ran
Under a car.
Today they will cry for you –
Tomorrow they will buy another dog.

JAMES MERRILL
My Father's Irish Setters

Always throughout his life
(The parts of it I knew)
Two or three would be racing
Up stairs and down hallways,
Whining to take us walking,
Or caked with dirt, resigning
Keen ears to bouts of talk –
Until his third, last wife
Put down her little foot.
That splendid, thoroughbred
Lineage was penned
Safely out of earshot:
Fed, of course, and watered,
But never let out to run.
'Dear God,' the new wife simpered,
Tossing her little head,
'Suppose they got run over –
Wouldn't *that* be the end?'

Each time I visited
(Once or twice a year)
I'd slip out, giving my word
Not to get carried away.
At the dogs' first sight of me
Far off – of anyone –
Began a joyous barking,
A russet-and-rapid-as-flame
Leaping, then whimpering lickings

Of face and hands through wire.
Like fire, like fountains leaping
With love and loyalty,
Put, were they, in safekeeping
By love, or for love's sake?
Dear heart, to love's own shame.
But loyalty transferred
Leaves famously slim pickings,
And no one's left to blame.

Divorced again, my father
(Hair white, face deeply scored)
Looked round and heaved a sigh.
The setters were nowhere.

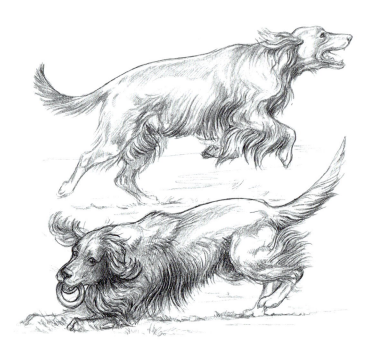

Fleet muzzle, soulful eye
Dead lo! these forty winters?
Not so. Tonight in perfect
Lamplit stillness begin
With updraft from the worksheet,
Leaping and tongues, far-shining
Hearths of our hinterland:
Dour chieftain, maiden pining
Away for that lost music,
Her harpist's wild red hair . . .
Dear clan of Ginger and Finn,
As I go through your motions
(As they go through me, rather)
Love follows, pen in hand.

☙

[141]

CLARISSE ALCOCK
Sally and Sambo

☙

As pretty a pair of cockers
As you could wish to meet,
Well trained and steady workers
In form both good and neat;

Coming their second season,
And of faultless pedigree,
Steady to fur and feather,
Real useful they should be.

Alas, their Master took a holiday,
And their distress was great,
All day they watched, and waited –
Sad and disconsolate.

But the Master had a wife
Unversed in sporting lore,
She noticed their depression
The dejected look they wore,

So she gave them liberty, and let
Them chase the rabbits through
The bracken and the furze until
The startled pheasants flew.

When the unsuspicious man returned,
And asked in words of cheer,
'Has everything been going well,
How are my cockers, dear?'

She smilingly replied 'I think
They are really clever things,
I loved to watch their antics
And the bunnies' scurryings.'

Then she wondered why he held his head,
Looked at her like that,
Paced up and down the room – and cried
'My cockers, Oh my hat!'

WILLIAM WORDSWORTH
Incident. Characteristic of a Favourite Dog

On his morning rounds the Master
Goes to learn how all things fare;
Searches pasture after pasture,
Sheep and cattle eyes with care;
And, for silence or for talk,
He hath comrades in his walk;
Four dogs, each pair of different breed,
Distinguished two for scent and two for speed.

See a hare before him started!
– Off they fly in earnest chase;
Every dog is eager-hearted,
All the four are in the race:
And the hare whom they pursue,
Hath an instinct what to do;
Her hope is near; no turn she makes;
But, like an arrow, to the river takes.

Deep the river was, and crusted
Thinly by a one night's frost;
But the nimble Hare hath trusted
To the ice, and safely crost;
She hath crost, and without heed
All are following at full speed,
When, lo! the ice so thinly spread,
Breaks – and the Greyhound, DART, is over head!

Better fate have PRINCE and SWALLOW –
See them cleaving to the sport!
MUSIC has no heart to follow,
Little MUSIC, she stops short.
She hath neither wish nor heart,
Hers is now another part:
A loving creature she, and brave!
And fondly strives her struggling friend to save.

From the brink her paws she stretches,
Very hands, as you would say!
And afflicting moans she fetches,
As he breaks the ice away.
For herself she hath no fears, –
Him alone she sees and hears, –
Makes efforts and complainings; nor gives o'er
Until her Fellow sank, and reappeared no more.

[143]

HENRY LAWSON

FROM

The Ballad of the Drover

. . . Now Harry speaks to Rover,
    The best dog on the plains,
And to his hardy horses,
    And strokes their shaggy manes;
'We've breasted bigger rivers
    When floods were at their height

Nor shall this gutter stop us
    From getting home to-night!'

The thunder growls a warning,
    The ghastly lightnings gleam,
As the drover turns his horses
    To swim the fatal stream.
But, oh! the flood runs stronger
    Then e'er it ran before;
The saddle-horse is failing,
    And only half-way o'er!

When flashes next the lightning,
    The flood's grey breast is blank,
And cattle dog and pack-horse
    Are struggling up the bank.
But in the lonely homestead
    The girl will wait in vain –
He'll never pass the stations
    In charge of stock again.

The faithful dog a moment
    Sits panting on the bank,
And then swims through the current
    To where his master sank.
And round and round in circles
    He fights with failing strength,
Till, borne down by the waters,
    The old dog sinks at length . . .

☙

JAMES REEVES
The Sea

The sea is a hungry dog,
Giant and grey.
He rolls on the beach all day.
With his clashing teeth and shaggy jaws
Hour upon hour he gnaws
The rumbling, tumbling stones,
And 'Bones, bones, bones, bones!'
The giant sea-dog moans,
Licking his greasy paws.

And when the night wind roars
And the moon rocks in the stormy cloud,
He bounds to his feet and snuffs and sniffs,
Shaking his wet sides over the cliffs,
And howls and hollos long and loud.

But on quiet days in May or June,
When even the grasses on the dune
Play no more their reedy tune,
With his head between his paws
He lies on the sandy shores,
So quiet, so quiet, he scarcely snores.

JOHN FREEMAN
The Hounds

Far off a lonely hound
Telling his loneliness all round
To the dark woods, dark hills, and darker sea;

And, answering, the sound
Of that yet lonelier sea-hound
Telling his loneliness to the solitary stars.

Hearing, the kennelled hound
Some neighbourhood and comfort found,
And slept beneath the comfortless high stars.

But that wild sea-hound
Unkennelled, called all night all round –
The unneighboured and uncomforted cold sea.

∽

[146]

W. SOMERVILLE
Hounds in Summer Weather

∽

To cooler shades
Lead forth the panting tribe; soon shalt thou find
The cordial breeze their fainting hearts revives;
Tumultuous soon they plunge into the stream,
There lave their reeking sides with greedy joy
Gulp down the flying wave, this way and that
From shore to shore they swim, while clamour loud
And wild uproar torments the troubled flood:
Then on the sunny bank they roll and stretch
Their dripping limbs, or else in wanton rings
Coursing around, pursuing and pursued,
The merry multitude disporting play.

∽

W. SOMERVILLE
The Foxhound

See there with countenance blithe
And with a courtly grin the fawning hound
Salutes thee cowering, his wide-opening nose
Upward he curls, and his large sloe black eyes
Melt in soft blandishments and humble joy;
His glossy skin, or yellow-pied or blue,
In lights or shades by Nature's pencil drawn,
Reflects the various tints, his ears and legs
Flecked here and there in gay enamelled pride,
Rival the speckled pard; his rush grown tail
O'er his broad back bends in an ample arch,
On shoulders clean, firm and upright he stands;

His round cat-foot, straight hams, and wide-spread
    thighs,
And his low dropping chest, confess his speed,
His strength, his wind, or on the steep hill,
Or far-extended plain; in every part
So well-proportioned, that the nicer skill
Of Phidias himself can't blame thy choice

ↄ

[148]

WILL OGILVIE
The White Hound

ↄ

The white hound runs at the head of the pack,
    And mute as a mouse is he,
And never a note he flings us back
    While the others voice their glee.
With nose to the ground he holds his line
    Be it over the plough or grass;
He sets a pace for the twenty-nine
    And won't let one of them pass.

The white hound comes from a home in Wales,
    Where they like them pale in hue
And can pick them up when the daylight fails
    And the first gold stars look through.
They can see them running on dark hill-sides
    If they speak to the scent or no,
And the snow-white hounds are welcome guides
    Where the wild Welsh foxes go.

The white hound runs with our dappled pack
  Far out behind him strung;
He shows the way to the tan-and-black
  But he never throws his tongue.
At times he leads by a hundred yards,
  But he's always sure and sound;
All packs, of course, have their picture cards,
  And ours is the old white hound.

The Master says he is far too fast
  For our stout, determined strain,
And the huntsman curses him – 'D–n and blast
  He's away by himself again!'
But the Field is glad when it sees him there,
  For we know when a fox is found
The pace will be hot and the riding rare
  In the track of the old white hound.

[149]

MICHAEL DRAYTON

FROM

Polyolbion

A horse of greater speed, nor yet a righter hound,
Not any where 'twixt Kent and Caledon is found.
Nor yet the level south can show a smoother race,
Whereas the ballow nag outstrips the winds in chase;
As famous in the west for matches yearly try'd,
As Garterley, possest of all the northern pride;

And on his match as much the Western horseman
  lays,
As the rank riding Scots upon their Galloways.
And as the western soil as sound a horse doth breed,
As doth the land that lies betwixt the Trent and
  Tweed:
No hunter, so, but finds the breeding of the west
The only kind of hounds for mouth, and nostril best;
That cold doth seldom fret, nor heat doth over-hail;
As standing in the flight, as pleasant on the trail;
Free hunting, eas'ly check'd, and loving every chase;
Straight running, hard and tough, of reasonable pace:
Not heavy, as that hound which Lancashire doth
  breed;
Nor as the northern kind, so light and hot of speed,
Upon the clearer chase, or on the foiled train,
Doth make the sweetest cry, in woodland or on plain.

[150]

G. J. WHYTE-MELVILLE

FROM

The Foxhound

On the straightest of legs and the roundest of feet
With ribs like a frigate his timbers to meet,
With a fashion and fling and a form so complete
That to see him dance over the flags is a treat.

WILLIAM SHAKESPEARE

FROM

The Taming of the Shrew
Act I Scene i

∽

Lord Huntsman, I charge thee, tender well my
hounds.
Breathe Merriman – the poor Cur is embossed –
And couple Clowder with the deep–mouthed brach.
Saw'st thou not, boy, how Silver made it good
At the hedge corner, in the coldest fault?
I would not lose the dog for twenty pound.
First Huntsman Why, Bellman is as good as he, my
Lord:
He cried upon it at the merest loss,
And twice today picked out the dullest scent;
Trust me, I take him for the better dog.
Lord Thou art a fool: if Echo were as fleet,
I would esteem him worth a dozen such.
But sup them well, and look unto them all;
Tomorrow I intend to hunt again.

∽

WILL OGILVIE
Alone with Hounds

A wall on a bank at the top of a plough –
Down a lane – and there's no one in front of us now!
Through a wood – then the upland with sky for its
      bounds!
We are out in the open, alone with the hounds!
    Alone with the hounds!
    The heart how it bounds
To that acme of rapture – alone with the hounds!

One moment they falter, then drive in swift flight;
There's a cap on the skyline to prove they are right!
A crash of rare music – Oh, sweetest of sounds
To the man on the stayer, alone with the hounds!
    Alone with the hounds!
    Their chorus resounds
In a song to our triumph, alone with the hounds!

Old grass and sound going, sweet country to ride;
Stone walls with sod tops that we take in our stride;
We would not have missed it for thousands of
      pounds –
This hour of fulfilment, alone with the hounds!
    Alone with the hounds!
    The scattered Field pounds
Far behind us; Fate leaves us alone with the hounds!

Oh, good horse and gallant, my rapture you share
As you top the tall fences with inches to spare,
To your pluck and condition the credit redounds

Of this gallop of gallops alone with the hounds!
  Alone with the hounds!
  Joy's uttermost bounds
We have reached as companions alone with the
  hounds!

∽

[153]

ANONYMOUS
Welsh Hunting 1869

'A most singular freak of a pack of hounds was witnessed at Pontypridd last week. The pack belonged to Mr George Thomas and were returning from the hunt, when, on coming into the town they ran into the shop of Mr Jenkins, grocer, and out again immediately, but with no less than five pounds of tallow candles, which they ravenously devoured in the street.' *Court Journal*, collected by Egerton Warburton.

∽

Where Jenkins in Wales,
Soap and candles retails,
The pack, in despite of their Whip,
They took up the scent
And away they went,
Each one with a tallow dip.

With a good seven pounds
These hungry hounds,
Away! and away! they go,
While joining the chase,
Followed Jenkins' best pace
Shouting Tallow! Tallow-Ho!

∽

WILLIAM SHAKESPEARE

FROM

A Midsummer Night's Dream
Act IV Scene i

‿

My hounds are bred out of the Spartan kind,
So flewed, so sanded; and their heads are hung
With ears that sweep away the morning dew;
Crook-kneed' and dew-lapped like Thessalian bulls;
Slow in pursuit, but matched in mouth like bells,
Each under each. A cry more tuneable
Was never halloo'd to, nor cheered with horn,
In Crete, in Sparta, nor in Thessaly. . .

‿

[155]

ANONYMOUS
The Eynsham Poaching Song

‿

Three Eynsham chaps went out one day
To Lord Abingdon's Manor they made their way,
They took their dogs to catch some game
And soon to Wytham Woods they came.

Chorus: Laddyo laddya foldiroll laddyo

They hadn't been long a-beating there
When one of the dogs put up a hare,
Up she jumped and away she sprang
At the very same time a pheasant ran.

Chorus . . .

They hadn't beat the Woods all through
When Barrett the keeper came in view.
When they saw the old bugger look
They made their way to Cassington Brook.

Chorus . . .

When we gets there it's full to the brim.
Well you'd have laughed to see us swim –
Ten feet of water if not more.
When we sets out our dogs came o'er.

Chorus . . .

Over hedges and ditches, gates and rails,
The dogs followed after, behind our heels –
If he'd have catched us, say what you will,
He'd have sent us all to Abingdon Goal.

Chorus . . .

ANONYMOUS
My Dogs and my Gun

What pleasures are found when in search of the game,
For steady's my dogs, and quite fatal's my aim;
So fatal's my aim, when my piece I let fly,
That down drops the bird, the poor victim must die;
I range o'er the fields from morn until night,
For my Dog and my Gun is my constant delight.

When Ceres and Phoebus are seen hand in hand,
With my pointers around me all under command,

I roam o'er the meadows and fields void of care,
No pastime on earth can with shooting compare.
With the game in my net I return home at night,
For my Dogs and my Gun is my constant delight.

New pleasures await me as home I retire,
For to please all my friends is my only desire;
My game I distribute and send them away,
Then with sparkling champaigne crown the sports
      of the day.
Thus cheerfully passes each day and each night,
For my Dogs and my Gun is my constant delight.

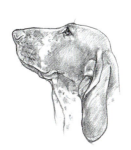

[157]

STEVIE SMITH

The Old Sweet Dove of Wiveton

The gray of this heavy day
Makes the green of the trees' leaves and the grass
    brighter
And the flowers of the chestnut tree whiter.
And whiter the flowers of the high cow-parsley.

So still is the air
So heavy the sky
You can hear the splash
Of the water falling from the green grass
As Red and Honey push by
The old dog
Gone away, gone hunting by the marsh bogs.

Happy the retriever dogs in their pursuit
Happy in bog-mud the busy foot.

[158]

STEPHEN VINCENT BENÉT

FROM

John Brown's Body

There was a man I knew near Pigeon Creek,
Who kept a kennel full of hunting-dogs,
Young dogs and old, smart hounds and silly hounds.
He'd sell the young ones every now and then,
Smart as they were and slick as they could run.
But the one dog he'd never sell or lend
Was an old half-deaf foolish-looking hound
You wouldn't think had sense to scratch a flea,
Unless the flea were old and sickly too.
Most days he used to lie beside the stove,
Or sleeping in a piece of sun outside.
Folks used to plague the man about that dog,
And he'd agree to everything they said:
'No – he ain't much on looks – or much on speed –

A young dog can outrun him any time,
Outlook him and outeat him and outleap him;
But, Mister, that dog's hell on a cold scent,
And, once he gets his teeth in what he's after,
He don't let go until he knows it's dead.'

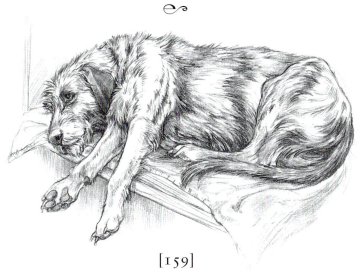

[159]

JOHN CLARE
FROM
February

The barking dogs, by lane and wood,
 Drive sheep afield from foddering ground;
And Echo, in her summer mood,
 Briskly mocks the cheering sound.
The flocks, as from a prison broke,
 Shake their wet fleeces in the sun,
While, following fast, a misty smoke
 Reeks from the moist grass as they run.

No more behind his master's heels
　The dog creeps on his winter pace;
But cocks his tail, and o'er the fields
　Runs many a wild and random chase,
Following, in spite of chiding calls,
　The startled cat with harmless glee,
Scaring her up the weed-green walls
　Or mossy mottled apple tree.

As crows from morning perches fly,
　He barks and follows them in vain;
E'en larks will catch his nimble eye,
　And off he starts and barks again,
With breathless haste and blinded guess,
　Oft following where the hare has gone,
Forgetting, in his joy's excess,
　His frolic puppy-days are done.

ROGER GARFITT
Blue

Memory on a peg
behind the door:

the slip-leash a live line
through my fingers

that floats on his shoulders'
running water

or knows their stiffening
the undertow

of another presence
in the hedgebank

still rancorous with fox.
Always that shock

as the hackles rise on
a waking dream,

an ancient line stands out
in the young dog.

Slip him, and I become
the outer ear,

the iris of his eye,
ready to shout

if he conjures a fox
as he stag-leaps

and salmons the long grass.
Enter the land

within the land, a light
and shadow land

whose denizens are quick
and changing shapes,

where the pheasant's wing spreads
into dead wood,

and riddles of brown earth
in the stubble

or clods of bleached-out grass
in the furrow

soon as our backs are turned
go haring off.

Enter the light and dark
of the duel,

the dog's dive and dolphin
over the ground,

a shoulder gleam breaking
the air's surface,

a slate gleam, night closing
with each new stride,

the hare's running rings, her
lucky numbers,

noughts and figures of eight,
a breathing space

won on every turn.
Enter the dark

of that other duel
he fought, the leash

an allegiance he held,
a last life line.

Sorrow still rives me that
I let him slip.

ALAN ROSS
Collie Romance

Sometimes at night I remember,
Long ago, on an autumn morning,
How she headed for the hills,
Took off without warning.

It was as though, across country,
She'd suddenly received signals,
Sounds unheard by the rest of us,
And had answered without fuss.

When, next day, she returned,
Coat matted, twigs in her fur,
Her look was half guilty, half sated,
Only her eyes burned.

ROGER ELKIN
A Dog's Eye View
❧

Took a dog's day snapping at heels, scratching at
    doors,
Nearly wagging my tail off to get in on this. Though I
    traded
Three good-dogs, Master didn't want me included,
    but Yan-man,
Smelling of linseed and with streakmeat smock,
    insisted – see
Him reflected in the background – though he even left
    me off
Till just before he cleaned out his brushes on the wall.
    That's
Why I'm walks-now up to him. The she-man standing
    in the door
Has whined two sunfuls about nothing but
    confinement. Suppose
It means no going here-boy all today. Again. She
    keeps turning
To sunlight the new fetch-boys she's brought in. Why
    won't she
Seek-out with me? Master's not himself either. He's
    not usually
So serious and pale, but there have been growlings
    long into
The fire with the grey old ones who clean behind my
    ears and
Uprdown with sit-begs; and now he's wearing his
    Sunday clothes,

And hat, even though it's a selling-day, and he's
     indoors.

I blame that other she-man. Since she came here,
     there's all
Those gnawbones littering the floor, or pushed just
     under the
Day-couch. Then by the see-self on the wall there's the
     gristly
String she walks her fingers on while she talks to her-
     self. Once
I could heel-boy and seek-out her eyes, but some-
     thing's come
Between us. Now I have to stand a walk-away to see
     her face.

I used to be Master's lap; but now she's the one that
     has him
Rough-and-tumbling, though you wouldn't know
     today. He isn't
Even good-boys with her, doesn't walk-smile; and his
     voice is
Like the big black book he speaks aloud each day.
     She's not sit-stay
For long, but throw-fetched, then stretched her length
     on the day-couch:
If she's got that after-eat-now feel, the big lie-down's
     close at hand.

To make things worse, there's woof of coming child.
     Hope it isn't
Master's brother's brat who pulls, prods and two-legs
     me, then yelps
When I nip, and mouth-wides when they bang me like

the rug. Couldn't
Stand that today. Though Yan-man's got a wag-tail
    likeness, it isn't
Worth getting famous to be framed by kids. Oh, Dog
    forbid.

[163]

OGDEN NASH
A Dog's Best Friend is his Illiteracy

It has been well said that quietness is what a Grecian
    urn is the still unravished bride of,
And that a door is what a dog is perpetually on the
    wrong side of.
I may add that a sachet is what many a housewife's
    linen is fragrantly entrusted to,
But that a cliché is what a dog owner must eventually
    get adjusted to.
Whether your visitor be Mr Belvedere or Bennett
    Cerf, what does he say when your dog greets
    him with Southern hospitality and salutes him
    all kissin' cousiny?

He says: 'He smells my dog on me, doesn't he?'
And he asks: 'How old is he?' and you say 'Twelve.'
    and he appraises Spot with the eye of an
    antiquarian,
And says: 'Seven twelves are eighty something, why
    Spot in human terms you're an octogenarian,'
But these two bromides are just the rattle before the
    strike,
Because then he says it's funny but he's noticed how
    often dogs and their masters look alike.
Such are the comments faced by dog owners from
    Peoria to Peshawar,
And frequently from a man who in canine terms is
    322 years old, and he is the spit and image of his
    own Chihuahua.
The only escape is to have something instead of dogs
    but whatever I substituted I should probably err,
And if I ended up with raccoons every guest would
    turn out to be a raccoonteur.

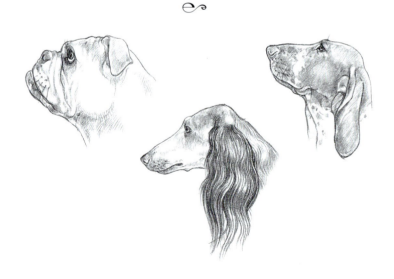

CHRISTOPHER REID
Two Dogs on a Pub Roof

ᕮᕲ

There are two dogs on a pub roof.
One's called Garth, the other Rolf.
Both are loud – but don't think they're all mouth.
I've been watching them and it's my belief
that they've been posted there, not quite on earth,
as emissaries of some higher truth
it's our job to get to the bottom of,
if only we can sort out the pith from the guff.
Garth's bark's no ordinary *woof, woof*:
it's a full-throttle affair, like whooping-cough,
a racking hack that shakes him from scruff
to tail in hour-long binges of holding forth
on all manner of obsessive stuff,
from pigeons and planes to not getting enough
to eat and so being ready to bite your head off.
He's whipped up in a perpetual froth
of indignation on his own behalf.
Poof! Dwarf! Oaf! Filth!
These and suchlike are among his chief
forms of salutation – and he means you, guv!
His whole philosophy, his pennyworth,
is 'All's enemy that's not self'
(with the provisional exception of his brother Rolf).
It's no joke and you don't feel inclined to laugh.
Rolf's even more frightening: his *arf! arf!*
seems designed to tear the sky in half,
every utterance an ultimate expletive,
every one a barbed shaft

aimed accurately at your midriff
and transfixing you with impotent wrath.
You and him. It bothers you both.
The thing's reciprocal, a north–south
axis that skewers the two of you like love.
You're David and Goliath, Peter and the Wolf,
Robin Hood and his Sheriff, Mutt and Jeff –
any ding-donging duo from history or myth
that's come to stand as a hieroglyph
for eternal foedom, non-stop strife,
the old Manichean fisticuffs
without which there'd be no story, no life,
and the whole cycle of birth, breath,
scoff, boff, graft, grief and death
would amount to so much waste of puff.
You're spiritual partners, hand in glove,
you and Rolfie, you and Garth,
you and the two of them up on that roof,
barking and hopping, acting tough,
flinging their taunts across the gulf
of the entire neighbourhood: *You lot down beneath!*
You got a diabolical nerve!
Who gave you permission to breathe?
This is our gaff! This is our turf!
Don't even think of crossing our path,
if you happen to value what remains of your health!
One false move and we'll show you teeth . . .
And so on. Of course, that's only a rough
translation, but it will more or less serve,
being at least the gist of the riff
that bores you mad and drives you stiff
all day long. Night, too. Nights, they work shifts.
One sleeps, while the other faces the brave
task of keeping the moon at a safe

distance and making sure the stars behave.
Which is why there are two of them. If
you've begun to wonder. As you no doubt have.
Then sometimes they'll mount an all-night rave,
Garth dancing with Rolf, Rolf with Garth –
though there's nothing queer about these two
    psychopaths
and you're the inevitable wallflower, on the shelf,
surplus to requirements. Only you can't stay aloof.
Like it or lump it, you're stuck in their groove.
The joint's jumping in every joist and lath
and nobody, but nobody, is going to leave.
You're as free an agent as the flame-fazed moth
that's in thrall, flamboyantly befuddled, and not
    fireproof.
You're party to the party, however loth.
You belong along. You're kin. You're kith.
You're living testimony to the preposition 'with'.
You're baby, bathwater and bath.
So don't dash out with your Kalashnikov
and hope to cut a definitive swathe
through the opposition. Don't throw that Molotov
cocktail. Put down that Swiss Army knife.
Stop spitting. Stop sputtering. Don't fluster. Don't
    faff.
And don't be so daft, naff, duff or uncouth
as to think you're calling anyone's bluff –
let alone that of the powers above –
by threatening to depart in a huff.
They are your world, where you live,
and this is what their telegraph
of yaps and yelps, their salvoes of snuff-
sneezes, their one-note arias, oath-
fests and dog-demagoguery, their throes of gruff

throat-flexing and guffaws without mirth
are meant to signify. And it's all for your behoof!
So thanks be to Garth, and thanks to Rolf –
those two soothsayers with their one sooth,
pontificating on that pub roof –
and thanks to the God who created them both
for your enlightenment and as proof of His ruth.

[165]

T. S. ELIOT
Pekes and Pollicles

THE Pekes and the Pollicles, everyone knows,
Are proud and implacable passionate foes;
It is always the same, wherever one goes.
And the Pugs and the Poms, although most people
     say
That they do not like fighting, yet once in a way,
They will now and again join in to the fray
And they
        Bark bark bark bark
        Bark Bark BARK BARK
     Until you can hear them all over the Park.

Now on the occasion of which I shall speak
Almost nothing had happened for nearly a week
(And that's a long time for a Pol or a Peke).
The big Police Dog was away from his beat –
I don't know the reason, but most people think
He'd slipped into the Wellington Arms for a drink –
And no one at all was about on the street
When a Peke and a Pollicle happened to meet.
They did not advance, or exactly retreat,
But they glared at each other, and scraped their hind
        feet,
And started to
            Bark Bark Bark bark
            Bark Bark BARK BARK
        Until you could hear them all over the Park.

Now the Peke, although people may say what they
        please,
Is no British dog, but a Heathen Chinese.
And so all the Pekes, when they heard the uproar,
Some came to the window, some came to the door;
There were surely a dozen, more likely a score.
And together they started to grumble and wheeze
In their huffery-snuffery Heathen Chinese.
But a terrible din is what Pollicles like,
For your Pollicle Dog is a dour Yorkshire tyke,
And his braw Scottish cousins are snappers and
        biters,
And every dog-jack of them notable fighters;
And so they stepped out, with their pipers in order,
Playing 'When the Blue Bonnets Came Over the
        Border.'
Then the Pugs and the Poms held no longer aloof,
But some from the balcony, some from the roof,

Joined in
To the din
With a

   Bark Bark Bark Bark
   Bark Bark BARK BARK
  Until you could hear them all over the Park.

Now when these bold heroes together assembled,
The traffic all stopped, and the Underground
  trembled,
And some of the neighbours were so much afraid
That they started to ring up the Fire Brigade.
When suddenly, up from a small basement flat,
Why who should stalk out but the *Great Rumpuscat.*
His eyes were like fireballs fearfully blazing,
He gave a great yawn, and his jaws were amazing;
And when he looked out through the bars of the
  area,
You never saw anything fiercer or hairier.
And what with the glare of his eyes and his yawning,
The Pekes and the Pollicles quickly took warning.
He looked at the sky and he gave a great leap –
And they every last one of them scattered like sheep.
And when the Police Dog returned to his beat,
There wasn't a single one left in the street.

ROGER McGOUGH
P.C. Plod versus
the Dalestreet Dogstrangler

For several months
Liverpool was held in the grip of fear
by a dogstrangler most devilish,
who roamed the streets after dark
looking for strays. Finding one
he would tickle it seductively
about the body to gain its confidence,
then lead it down a deserted backstreet
where he would strangle the poor brute.
Hardly a night passed without somebody's
faithful fourlegged friend being dispatched
to that Golden Kennel in the sky.

The public were warned:
At the very first sign
of anything suspicious,
ring Canine-nine-nine.

Nine o'clock on the evening of January 11th
sees P.C. Plod on the corner
of Dale St and Sir Thomas St
disguised as a Welsh collie.
It is part of a daring plan to apprehend the strangler.
For though it is a wet and moonless night,
Plod is cheered in the knowledge
that the whole of the Liverpool City Constabulary
is on the beat that night disguised as dogs.

Not ten minutes earlier, a pekinese
(Policewoman Hodges)
had scampered past on her way to Clayton Square.

For Plod, the night passed uneventfully
and so in the morning he was horrified to learn
that no less than fourteen policemen and police-
       women
had been tickled and strangled during the night.

    The public were horrified
    The Commissioner aghast
    Something had to be done
    And fast.

P.C. Plod (wise as a brace of owls)
met the challenge magnificently
and submitted an idea so startling in its vision
so audacious in its conception
that the Commissioner gasped
before ordering all dogs in the city
to be thereinafter disguised as fuzz.
The plan worked
and the dogstrangler was heard of no more.

Cops and mongrels
like P.C.s in a pod
To a grateful public
Plod was God.

So next time you're up in Liverpool
take a closer look
at the policemen on pointduty,
he might well be a copper spaniel.

❧

[167]

WILLIAM BEAUMONT
FROM
Liquorice
❧

John William Cawverly sowld me a pup
For a pint o' best bitter an' hauf-a-crown;
I spent a twelvemonth i' bringin' him up,
An' he spent a twelvemonth i' gettin' me down.

His legs were a whippet's, his tail were a peke's,
His head a retriever's – he seemed built for sports –
He'd a spot o' dalmatian in both of his cheeks,
So I christened him Liquorice – he were all sorts.

He grew an' he grew, for he did nowt but eyt,
– Whativver I gave him, he wadn't refuse –
He cost me a fortune i' biscuits an' meyt,
An' he cost me another i' slippers an' shoes.

Since I got him a licence, he's worried two cats,
He's nibbled at t' postman, an' Joe Willie Sykes;
He's riven a rug an' a couple o' mats –
He thinks it's a licence to do as he likes!

He fair took a fancy to young Sammy Kaye –
A fancy that led him to chew Sammy's leg;
An' now, ivvery time Sammy comes up our way,
T' dog's nobbut to see him, to sit up an' beg.

One neet when a burglar were prowlin' about,
I jamp out o' bed as he tried to break in;
As I tiptoed thra t' bedroom, I gave sich a shout –
For Liquorice wakkened an' got me bi t' shin!

I once tried to lose him; I took him ten mile,
An' left him i-rabbitin', ovver on t' moor;
But when I got home, he were sittin' i' style,
Laughin' his head off, outside mi font-door.

I decided to sell him; a customer came,
– A pleasant young feller, wi' manners so nice,
But t' dog chased him off when he rumbled mi
     game –
He seemed to go mad when I mentioned mi price.

An' monny a time, as I look at th' owld lad,
I shudder to think just what kind of a job
He'd ha' made o' yond youngster who answered mi
     ad,
If I'd asked him a dollar, astead o' ten bob!

⟳

TED HUGHES

Roger the Dog

Asleep he wheezes at his ease,
He only wakes to scratch his fleas.

He hogs the fire, he bakes his head,
As if it were a loaf of bread.

He's just a sack of snoring dog,
You can lug him like a log.

You can roll him with your foot,
He'll stay snoring where he's put.

I take him out for exercise,
He rolls in cowclap up to his eyes.

He will not race, he will not romp,
He saves his strength for gobble and chomp.

He'll work as hard as you could wish,
Emptying his dinner dish.

Then flops flat, and digs down deep,
Like a miner, into sleep.

OLWEN WAY
To an Old Dog by the Fire
❧

MASSIVE content, fulfilment and slow peace
Fire-glow enwraps, embalms –
The warmth plays tenderly on your old ease
Old-age-white muzzle and great calloused limbs
A solemn largo, a slow movement's peace.

Dear Dane, the fire's vitality plays well,
Lending you lease of life
To shore up all that's left in you to tell
With your dark eyes, how love will still contrive
To outstrip in spirit that great body's shell.

❧

JOE WALKER

Waiting up for Master

Asleep? Not they – for, as you close the door,
Hark to a patter on the parquet floor,
And little squeals of unalloyed delight;
'At last you're back; you're very late to-night.
We thought you'd never come.' The greetings cease,
Whilst eager glances scan the mantelpiece.
Ecstatic silence! as you turn to take
Down from its resting-place, then slowly break
The ritual biscuit into equal shares –
Jock's on the mat, and Peter's by the stairs.
The last crumb finished, with reluctant tread

Each seeks the comfort of his cosy bed
(Viewing the other with suspicious frown,
To make quite certain that he's settling down).
'Now, not a sound! Good-night!' Four amber eyes
Strive to convey their sad – nay, pained surprise.
Out goes the light; upstairs you softly creep.
. . . Two little sighs . . . Two happy dogs asleep.

[171]

THOM GUNN
Yoko

All today I lie in the bottom of the wardrobe
feeling low but sometimes getting up
to moodily lumber across rooms
and lap from the toilet bowl, it is so sultry
and then I hear the noise of firecrackers again
all New York is jaggedy with firecrackers today
and I go back to the wardrobe gloomy
trying to void my mind of them.
I am confused, I feel loose and unfitted.

At last deep in the stairwell I hear a tread,
it is him, my leader, my love.
I run to the door and listen to his approach.
Now I can smell him, what a good man he is,
I love it when he has the sweat of work on him,
as he enters I yodel with happiness,
I throw my body up against his, I try to lick his lips,
I care about him more than anything.

After we eat we go for a walk to the piers.
I leap into the standing warmth, I plunge into
the combination of old and new smells.
Here on a garbage can at the bottom, so interesting,
what sister or brother I wonder left this message I
      sniff.
I too piss there, and go on.
Here a hydrant there a pole
here's a smell I left yesterday, well that's disappointing
but I piss there anyway, and go on.

I investigate so much that in the end
it is for form's sake only, only a drop comes out.

I investigate tar and rotten sandwiches, everything,
      and go on.

And here a dried old turd, so interesting
so old, so dry, yet so subtle and mellow.
I can place it finely, I really appreciate it,
a gold distant smell like packed autumn leaves in
      winter
reminding me how what is rich and fierce when
      excreted
becomes weathered and mild
                         but always interesting
and reminding me of what I have to do.

My leader looks on and expresses his approval.

I sniff it well and later I sniff the air well
a wind is meeting us after the close July day
rain is getting near too but first the wind.

Joy, joy,
being outside with you, active, investigating it all,
with bowels emptied, feeling your approval
and then running on, the big fleet Yoko,
my body in its excellent black coat never lets me
     down,
returning to you (as I always will, you know that)
and now
       filling myself out with myself, no longer
    confused,
my panting pushing apart my black lips, but
    unmoving,
I stand with you braced against the wind.

MAX FATCHEN
Night Walk

What are you doing away up there
On your great long legs in the lonely air?
  Come down here, where the scents are sweet,
  Swirling around your great, wide feet.

How can you know of the urgent grass
And the whiff of the wind that will whisper and pass
  Or the lure of the dark of the garden hedge
  Or the trail of a cat on the road's black edge?

What are you doing away up there
On your great long legs in the lonely air?
  You miss so much at your great, great height
  When the ground is full of the smells of night.

Hurry then, quickly, and slacken my lead
For the mysteries speak and the messages speed
  With the talking stick and the stone's slow mirth
  That four feet find on the secret earth.

[173]

HOWARD NEMEROV
Walking the Dog

Two universes mosey down the street
Connected by love and a leash and nothing else.
Mostly I look at lamplight through the leaves
While he mooches along with tail up and snout
    down
Getting a secret knowledge through the nose
Almost entirely hidden from my sight.

We stand while he's enraptured by a bush
Till I can't stand our standing any more
And haul him off; for our relationship
Is patience balancing to this side tug
And that side drag; a pair of symbionts
Contented not to think each other's thoughts.

What else we have in common's what he taught,
Our interest in shit. We know its every state
From steaming fresh through stink to nature's way
Of sluicing it downstreet dissolved in rain
Or drying it to dust that blows away.
We move along the street inspecting it.

His sense of it is keener far than mine,
And only when he finds the place precise
He signifies by sniffing urgently
And circles thrice about, and squats, and shits,
Whereon we both with dignity walk home
And just to show who's master I write the poem.

[174]

ELEANOR FARJEON
Outside

He's pulling on his boots!
He's going out again –
Out to the world of roots,
The whipping wind and rain,
The stinging sun that tells
On bristles and in blood,
Out to the place of smells,
And things that move, and mud;
Out where, to run a race,
Is not to hit a wall;

Out to the time of chase!
Will he whistle and call?
He's looking for his stick,
He's – Hark! his glorious shout!
I'm coming quick-quick-quick!
We're going out! We're *Out*.

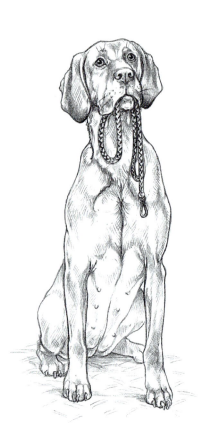

HAROLD MONRO

Dog

O little friend, your nose is ready; you sniff,
Asking for that expected walk,
(Your nostrils full of the happy rabbit-whiff)
And almost talk.

. . .

We are going *Out*. You know the pitch of the word,
Probing the tone of thought as it comes through fog
And reaches by devious means (half-smelt, half-
       heard)
The four-legged brain of a walk-ecstatic dog.

Out through the garden your head is already low.
You are going your walk, you know,
And your limbs will draw
Joy from the earth through the touch of your padd
       paw.

Now, sending a little look to us behind,
Who follow slowly the track of your lovely play,
You fetch our bodies forward away from mind
Into the light and fun of your useless day.

. . .

Thus, for your walk we took ourselves, and went
Out by the hedge, and tree, to the open ground.
You ran, in delightful strata of wafted scent,

Over the hill without seeing the view;
Beauty is hinted through primitive smells to you:
And that ultimate Beauty you track is but rarely
        found.

Home . . . and further joy will be waiting there:
Supper full of the lovely taste of bone.
You lift up your nose again, and sniff, and stare
For the rapture known

Of the quick wild gorge of food, then the still lie-
        down;
While your people will talk above you in the light
Of candles, and your dreams will merge and drown
Into the bed-delicious hours of night.

JUDITH ADAMS
Walking the Dogs
℮

This is no common
Ritual to be out again on the
Headlands, and hoarfrost.
To follow pathways into mist
and circle a cursive language
across the cold hills.

To go early is to sniff
the still warm nuggets of
night where the relaxed
body of the fox has woven
red down the long
slope towards the woods.

They bounce back towards me
checking that I am as happy
and coming along the ridge.
The sheep dog douses himself
in deer dropping, seductive as
if it were Chanel No. 5.

Turning towards home
and away from the wind
I call out to them
Finally they rise out of the
echo of their own names
Ears flapping towards me.

℮

LOUIS MacNEICE
Dogs in the Park

The precise yet furtive etiquette of dogs
Makes them ignore the whistle while they talk
In circles round each other, one-man bonds
Deferred in pauses of this man-made walk
To open vistas to a past of packs

That raven round the stuccoed terraces
And scavenge at the mouth of Stone Age caves;
What man proposes dog on his day disposes
In litter round both human and canine graves,
Then lifts his leg to wash the gravestones clean,

While simultaneously his eyes express
Apology and contempt; his master calls
And at the last and sidelong he returns,
Part heretic, part hack, and jumps and crawls
And fumbles to communicate and fails.

And then they leave the park, the leads are snapped
On to the spiky collars, the tails wag
For no known reason and the ears are pricked
To search through legendary copse and crag
For legendary creatures doomed to die
Even as they, the dogs, were doomed to live.

[178]

JOHN BENNETT
Walkies

He scorns my gait
That eager pup,
Content to wait
Till I catch up.
There isn't room
For any doubt
Who's taking whom
When we are out!

[179]

PAULINE ANDERSON
Our Puppy

Tail a-wagging, throaty barks,
Hoping to be heard,
You stand there so expectantly
Hanging on our words.
Rolling on your back now
Paws waving in the air,
You want to have your tummy rubbed
By anyone who's there.

You scramble to your feet again,
Run quickly to the door,
Sit up on your back legs now
As you have done before,
You beg for a lump of sugar,
We place it on your nose,
You toss it up and catch it
Then down your throat it goes.

Playing now with your rubber ball
As you've done since first we bought it,
Then round and round you chase your tail
But what would you do if you caught it?
Our frisky little puppy
Full of playfulness and fun
Keeps everybody busy
His demands are never done.

[180]

F. CONQUEST

A Stern Story

I have a little puppy, and he often runs around
  And tries to catch the tail he hasn't got;
He always seems surprised and hurt to see it can't be
      found,
  But knowing men assure me he is not.

Because he was so little that his baby eyes were shut,
  He never saw it, so he never knew
How very nice and long it was before they had it cut,
  And only left him just an inch or two.

They say he looks more handsome and is saved a lot
      of woes;
  One can't step on a tail that is no more;
Hot cinders cannot burn it, and, as every Manx cat
      knows,
  It can't get caught within a slamming door.
But he quivers with excitement from his head down
      to his toes
  When I light back from the station with my bag,
And he wriggles from his little stump right to his little
      nose,
  And I *know* he'd like a longer tail to wag.

IVY EASTWICK

The Puppy Chased the Sunbeam

The puppy chased the sunbeam
All around the house –
He thought it was a bee,
Or a little golden mouse.
He thought it was a spider
On a little silver string;
He thought it was a butterfly
Or some such flying thing;
He thought – but oh! I cannot tell you
Half the things he thought
As he chased the sparkling sunbeam
Which – just – would – not – be caught

[182]

V. SACKVILE-WEST
FROM
The Land

Nor shall you for your fields neglect your stock;
Spring is the season when the young things thrive,
Having the kindly months before them. Lambs,
Already sturdy, straggle from the flock; . . .
. . . Round collie puppies, on the sunny steps,
Buffet each other with their duffer paws
And pounce at flies, and nose the plaited skep,
And with tucked tail slink yelping from the hive . . .

[183]

OGDEN NASH
For a Good Dog

My little dog ten years ago
Was arrogant and spry,
Her backbone was a bended bow
For arrows in her eye.
Her step was proud, her bark was loud,
Her nose was in the sky,
But she was ten years younger then,
And so, by God, was I.

Small birds on stilts along the beach
Rose up with piping cry,
And as they flashed beyond her reach
I thought to see her fly.
If natural law refused her wings,
That law she would defy,
For she could hear unheard-of things,
And so, at times, could I.

Ten years ago she split the air
To seize what she could spy;
Tonight she bumps against a chair,
Betrayed by milky eye.
She seems to pant, Time up, time up!
My little dog must die,
And lie in dust with Hector's pup;
So, presently, must I.

ROBERT SOUTHEY
To a Favourite Spaniel

Ah, poor companion! when thou followedst last
    Thy master's footsteps to the gate
Which closed for ever on him, thou didst lose
Thy truest friend, and none was left to plead
For the old age of brute fidelity.
But fare thee well! Mine is no narrow creed;
And He who gave thee being did not frame

The mystery of life to be the sport
Of merciless man! There is another world
For all that live and move – a better one!
Where the proud bipeds, who would fain confine
Infinite Goodness to the little bounds
Of their own charity, may envy thee!

[185]

HARRY GHISI
Dogs

I have seen the pacing dogs, pacing on
the verge of running, I have seen the urgency
of their measured trot. I understand the one intention
held behind their sharp eyes, and I
know its cause.

They're brought here by families
from out of town, made to wait outside some café,
abandoned to wander lost in the alleyways.

Winter Venice is an endless maze, circled
by a cold sea; consolingly carless and safe.
But these betrayed dogs search tirelessly,
their puzzled eyes crushed by worry. They
never lose hope.

I have seen abandoned
children, puzzled by the same questions, driven by
the same needs, looking desperately out
of the eyes of men, behind which they circle still,
lost in a darker labyrinth.

JENNY JOSEPH
Dog Body and Cat Mind

The dog body and cat mind
Lay in the room with the fire dying.
Will went out and locked the door.
Then the dog started howling.
He went to the door and scratched at it.
He went to the window and barked at it.
He prowled round the room sniffing and whining
Put his nose to the wainscot and whimpered in the
    dust
The dog body and the cat mind
Locked in a room with the fire dying
And the dog would not lie down and be still.

He hurtled his shoulders against the wall:
He upset the cat's food and stepped in it,
He barked hard at his wild reflection
On the blank window. And he banged his head
Until it ached, on the stone floor,
And still could not lie down and be still.

Then, worn out with howling and scratching and
    banging
The dog flopped to a weary defeated sleep

And then the cat got up and started walking.

WILLIAM WATSON
An Epitaph

His friends he loved. His fellest earthly foes –
Cats – I believe he did but feign to hate.
My hand will miss the insinuated nose,
Mine eyes the tail that wagged contempt at Fate.

THOMAS CAMPBELL
Poor Dog Tray

On the green banks of Shannon when Sheelah was
    nigh,
No blithe Irish lad was so happy as I;
No harp like my own could so cheerily play,
And wherever I went was my poor dog Tray.

Poor dog! he was faithful and kind to be sure,
And he constantly loved me although I was poor;
When the sour-looking folk sent me heartless away,
I had always a friend in my poor dog Tray.

When the road was so dark, and the night was so
    cold,
And Pat and his dog were grown weary and old,
How snugly we slept in my old coat of grey,
And he lick'd me for kindness – my old dog Tray.

Though my wallet was scant I remember'd his case,
Nor refused my last crust to his pitiful face;
But he died at my feet on a cold winter day,
And I play'd a sad lament for my poor dog Tray.

PINDAR

The Old Shepherd's Dog

The old shepherd's dog, like his master, was grey,
His teeth all departed and feeble his tongue;
Yet where'er Corin went he was followed by Tray,
Thus happy through life they did hobble along.

When fatigued on the grass the shepherd would lie
For a nap in the sun, 'midst his slumbers so sweet
His faithful companion crawled constantly nigh,
Placed his head on his lap, or laid down at his feet.

When winter was heard on the hill or the plain,
When torrents descended and cold was the wind;
If Corin went forth 'mid the tempest and rain,
Tray scorned to be left in the chimney behind.

At length, in the straw, Tray made his last bed –
For vain against death is the stoutest endeavour –
To lick Corin's hand he reared up his weak head,
Then fell back, closed his eyes, and ah! closed
    them forever.

Not long after Tray did the shepherd remain,
Who oft o'er his grave with true sorrow would bend;
And when dying, was feebly heard the poor swain,
'Oh, bury me, neighbours, beside my old friend!'

SIR HENRY NEWBOLT
Fidele's Grassy Tomb

ᗧᔕ

The Squire sat propped in a pillowed chair,
His eyes were alive and clear of care,
But well he knew that the hour was come
To bid good-bye to his ancient home.

He looked on garden, wood, and hill,
He looked on the lake, sunny and still:
The last of earth that his eyes could see
Was the island church of Orchardleigh.

The last that his heart could understand
Was the touch of the tongue that licked his hand:
'Bury the dog at my feet,' he said,
And his voice dropped, and the Squire was dead.

Now the dog was a hound of the Danish breed,
Staunch to love and strong at need:
He had dragged his master safe to shore
When the tide was ebbing at Elsinore.

From that day forth, as reason would,
He was named 'Fidele,' and made it good:
When the last of the mourners left the door
Fidele was dead on the chantry floor.

They buried him there at his master's feet,
And all that heard of it deemed it meet:
The story went the round for years,
Till it came at last to the Bishop's ears.

Bishop of Bath and Wells was he,
Lord of the lords of Orchardleigh;
And he wrote to the Parson the strongest screed
That Bishop may write or Parson read.

The sum of it was that a soulless hound
Was known to be buried in hallowed ground:
From scandal sore the Church to save
They must take the dog from his master's grave.

The heir was far in a foreign land,
The Parson was wax to my Lord's command:
He sent for the Sexton and bade him make
A lonely grave by the shore of the lake.

The Sexton sat by the water's brink
Where he used to sit when he used to think:
He reasoned slow, but he reasoned it out,
And his argument left him free from doubt.

'A Bishop,' he said, 'is the top of his trade;
But there's others can give him a start with the spade:
Yon dog, he carried the Squire ashore,
And a Christian couldn't ha' done no more.'

The grave was dug; the mason came
And carved on stone Fidele's name;
But the dog that the Sexton laid inside
Was a dog that never lived or died.

So the Parson was praised, and the scandal stayed,
Till, a long time after, the church decayed,
And, laying the floor anew, they found
In the tomb of the Squire the bones of a hound.

As for the Bishop of Bath and Wells
No more of him the story tells;
Doubtless he lived as a Prelate and Prince,
And died and was buried a century since.

And whether his view was right or wrong
Has little to do with this my song;
Something we owe him, you must allow;
And perhaps he has changed his mind by now.

The Squire in the family chantry sleeps,
The marble still his memory keeps:
Remember, when the name you spell,
There rest Fidele's bones as well.

For the Sexton's grave you need not search,
'Tis a nameless mound by the island church:
An ignorant fellow, of humble lot –
But he knew one thing that a Bishop did not.

MICHAEL DRAYTON
FROM
Tenth Eclogues

ℰ

He called his dog (that sometime had the praise),
Whitefoot, well known to all that keep the plain,
That many a wolf had worried in his days,
A better cur there never followed swain;
    Which, though as he his master's sorrows knew,
    Wagged his cut tail, his wretched plight to rue.

'Poor cur,' quoth he, and him therewith did stroke;
'Go to our cote, and there thyself repose,
Thou with thine age, my heart with sorrow broke,
Be gone, e'er death my restless eyes do close.
    The time is come thou must thy master leave,
    Whom the vile world shall never more deceive.'

ℰ

NORMAN MacCAIG

Angus's Dog

Black collie, do you remember yourself?

Do you remember your name was Mephistopheles,
though (as if you were only a little devil)
everyone called you Meph?

You'd chase everything – sea gulls, motor cars,
jet planes. (It's said you once set off
after a lightning flash.) Half over a rock,
you followed the salmon fly arcing
through the bronze water. You loved everything
except rabbits – though
you grinned away under the bed
when your master came home
drink taken. How you'd lay your head
on a visitor's knee and look up, so soulfully,
like George Eliot playing Sarah Bernhardt.

... Black Meph, how can you remember yourself
in that blank no-time, no-place where
you can't even greet your master
though he's there too?

C. DAY-LEWIS
Sheepdog Trials in Hyde Park
ᐁ

A shepherd stands at one end of the arena.
Five sheep are unpenned at the other. His dog runs
    out
In a curve to behind them, fetches them straight to the
    shepherd,
Then drives the flock round a triangular course
Through a couple of gates and back to his master;
    two
Must be sorted there from the flock, then all five
    penned.
Gathering, driving away, shedding and penning
Are the plain words for the miraculous game.

An abstract game. What can the sheepdog make of
    such
Simplified terrain? – no hills, dales, bogs, walls,
    tracks,
Only a quarter-mile plain of grass, dumb crowds
Like crowds on hoardings around it, and behind them
Traffic or mounds of lovers and children playing.
Well, the dog is no landscape-fancier; his whole
    concern
Is with his master's whistle, and of course
With the flock – sheep are sheep anywhere for him.

The sheep are the chanciest element. Why, for
    instance,
Go through this gate when there's on either side of it

No wall or hedge but huge and viable space?
Why not eat the grass instead of being pushed around
    it?
Like blobs of quicksilver on a tilting board
The flock erratically runs, dithers, breaks up,
Is reassembled: their ruling idea is the dog;
And behind the dog, though they know it not yet, is a
    shepherd.

The shepherd knows that time is of the essence
But haste calamitous. Between dog and sheep
There is always an ideal distance, a perfect angle;
But these are constantly varying, so the man
Should anticipate each move through the dog, his
    medium.
The shepherd is the brain behind the dog's brain,
But his control of dog, like dog's of sheep,
Is never absolute – that's the beauty of it.

For beautiful it is. The guided missiles,
The black-and-white angels follow each quirk and
    jink of
The evasive sheep, play grandmother's steps behind
    them,
Freeze to the ground, or leap to head off a straggler
Almost before it knows that it wants to stray,
As if radar-controlled. But they are not machines –
You can feel them feeling mastery, doubt, chagrin:
Machines don't frolic when their job is done.

What's needfully done in the solitude of sheep-runs –
Those tough, real tasks – becomes this stylized game,
A demonstration of intuitive wit
Kept natural by the saving grace of error.

To lift, to fetch, to drive, to shed, to pen
Are acts I recognize, with all they mean
Of shepherding the unruly, for a kind of
Controlled woolgathering is my work to.

[194]

GARY PAULSEN
Dogsong

Come, see my dogs.

    Out before me
    they go,
    in the long line to the sea.
    Out they go.

Come, see my dogs.

    They carry me
    into all things, all things I will be;
    all things that will come to me
    will come to my dogs.
    I stand on the earth and I sing.

Come, see my dogs.

See them, see them
in the smoke of my life,
in the eyes of my children,
in the sound of my feet,
in the dance of my words.
I stand on the earth and I sing.

Come, see my dogs.

My dogs are what lead me,
they are what move me.
See my dogs in the steam,
in the steam of my life.
They are me.

Come, see my dogs.

I was nothing before them,
no man
and no wife.
Without them, no life,
no girl-woman breathing
no song.

Come, see my dogs.

With them I ran,
ran north to the sea.
I stand by the sea and I sing.
I sing of my hunts
and of Oogruk.

Come, see my dogs.

Out before me they go.
Out before me they curve
in the long line out
before me
they go, I go, we go. They are me.

❧

[195]

DAVID BLUNKETT
Teddy

❧

He was a gentle giant of a dog
Running magnificent through the woods
A huge branch clamped between his teeth.

He was a soft lion of a dog,
Full of sniffs and a nuzzling nose,
Touching against the hand
To say thank you for walks
And for fondling of ears.

He was a 'Guinness Book of Records' dog
First ever in the Chamber
Enduring the noise and the bad behaviour
Of the 'Schoolboys'
And the medieval ritual of the Mother of
    Parliaments.

He was a TV star dog
Sleeping through 'Question Time'
Lifting his head only when it was time to go,
And bringing a smile to millions
And joy to those who knew him well.

A child could climb upon his back
Or pull his ears without fear or threat
For Teddy was a dog of love, you see,
Who cared for others as he cared for me.

Guiding me wherever I needed to be
Full of keeness, enthusiasm and love of life
Working to a record age
And giving of his best wherever we might be.

Being superb, my guide dog gave his all
In those twelve years you see
And all of us who knew him
Will remember him with gratitude
And with love and affection.

ANONYMOUS
A Dog's Tombstone

TRANSLATED FROM THE GREEK BY
The Right Honourable Lord Hailsham

❧

This tombstone, stranger passing near,
Shows that a little dog lies here:
Tells how a master's loving hand
Carved these words and heaped this sand.
Smile if you please. But, when you die
Shall you be mourned as much as I?

❧

GEOFFREY DEARMER
Love the Usurer

❧

Lightly, oh Usurer, and without misgiving
From the heart's store we paid and like one man.
To pay was easy whilst our friend was living,
But it goes on, your fixed instalment plan.
Our little friend is dead. His trivial habits
Are trivial now no longer. He has gained
Something he lacked when after rats or rabbits
When the earth sang with smells and it had rained.

Oh Usurer, why grant us no release,
Can he for whom we sorrow benefit?
To love is to court grief that will not cease,
Oh Usurer, what is the sense of it?
We could not possibly be paying more
If he'd had longer legs and less than four.

⁒

LAURENCE WHISTLER
Folly: At the Death of a Dog
⁒

To care so much for one who gave but small
Answers to love, yet gave them, after his kind,
Completely – wild with pleasure in the giving.

To grieve so much, when he, whom love had whistled
Out of his cramped, regretless, primitive world,
Harked back, before his time, to brutal dying.

To want so much that somehow (life gone by)
This brief encounter, by the world forgotten,
Should somewhere be remembered – and be valued –
And hold one spark through all the blaze of being –
And, humbly, be.

⁒

CECIL FLOERSHEIM
In Memory of my Dog

ℰ๏

Beside your grave no prayer was said,
   Nor solemn tribute borne
By men who reverence the dead
   In whom themselves they mourn.

No life they promised void of stress,
   No heaven to you bequeathed,
Whose blue is but its emptiness,
   Whose heights life never breathed.

Yet here where nought enduring proves,
   That made your little day,
Where man must leave the things he loves,
   Or see them snatched away,

Remembering the joy you gave,
   Dear Comrade, heavy-souled
I stand alone beside your grave,
   And feel the sunshine cold.

And thinking of life's brief delight
   That we no more shall share;
Perform the unavailing rite,
   And say the unsaid prayer.

ℰ๏

JOE WALKER
Buried Treasure

I turn the earth, and there – disclosed to view –
The buried treasure, still of ivory hue;
It must have been the last bone that he had.

I see him trotting business-like and glad
To find a hiding-place for this great prize
Safe from the glance of prying human eyes,
Then hastening houseward with suspicious mien;
'Now don't pretend you know where I have been!'
Had he forgotten where his treasure lay?
Would he have come – perhaps the very day . . . ?
I cover it again. A tiny bit
Of something else is buried, too, with it.

ॐ

[201]

RUDYARD KIPLING
Four-Feet

ॐ

I have done mostly what most men do,
And pushed it out of my mind;
But I can't forget, if I wanted to,
Four-Feet trotting behind.

Day after day, the whole day through –
Wherever my road inclined –
Four-feet said, 'I am coming with you!'
And trotted along behind.

Now I must go by some other round, –
Which I shall never find –
Somewhere that does not carry the sound
Of Four-Feet trotting behind.

ॐ

BIOGRAPHICAL
INDEX OF POETS

References are to poem numbers.

JUDITH ADAMS 89, 176
Suffolk-born children's author and teacher now living in Pennsylvania.

ALLAN AHLBERG 74
Contemporary British writer of books and poems for children, well-known for 'The Jolly Post Office'.

CLARISSE ALCOCK 46, 141
Published 1940.

PAULINE ANDERSON 179
Member of a Cambridge poetry group.

ANONYMOUS 12, 34, 40, 56, 59, 66, 76, 84, 107, 112, 123, 153, 155, 156, 196

SIR EDWIN ARNOLD (1832–1904) 64
Author of *The Light of Asia* and other poems resulting from time spent in India.

MATTHEW ARNOLD (1822–88) 86
Poet and critic, educated at Rugby (where his father was head-master) and Oxford. Private Secretary to Lord Lansdowne and an Inspector of Schools.

PETER ARTHUR (1915–2000) 91
Architect and published poet. Former member of a Cambridge poetry group.

LES BARKER 71
Popular folk poet, known for his humorous readings.

ELIZABETH BARRETT BROWNING (1806–61) 19, 118
Wife of Robert, prolific poetess and famous for her affection for her dog Flush.

KATHLEEN BARROW 68
Contemporary writer.

WILLIAM BEAUMONT 167
Published 1973.

STEPHEN VINCENT BENÉT (1898–1943) 158
American poet, wrote 'John Brown's Body' about the American Civil War.

JOHN BENNETT (b. 1938) 178
American writer of novels, stories and poetry.

THE BIBLE 115

DAVID BLUNKETT (b. 1947) 195
Labour MP, 1987–; Secretary of State for Education 1997–. Uses a seeing-eye dog.

GEORGE GORDON, LORD BYRON (1788–1824) 53
Poet, born in London, his father died when he was three and he was brought up in difficult circumstances, not helped by being lame. Educated at Harrow and Trinity College Cambridge, he eventually succeeded to his great-uncle's title and estates. He spent much of his life abroad and involved himself in the Greek struggle for liberation from Turkey.

THOMAS CAMPBELL (1777–1844) 188
Scottish poet who originally studied law but then settled for a
literary life. Possibly his best-known poem is 'The Battle of the
Baltic.'

PATRICK CHALMERS 24, 58, 125
Early twentieth-century poet, published in *Punch* and else-
where.

BRENDA CHAMBERLAIN (1912–71) 110
Welsh critic and writer.

JOHN CLARE (1793–1864) 159
Poet of rural life from a poor background; became insane in
1837.

F. CONQUEST 180
Published in *Punch*.

FRANCES CORNFORD (1886–1960) 77
The granddaughter of Charles Darwin and a friend of the poet
Rupert Brooke.

WILLIAM COWPER (1731–1800) 44, 50, 102, 103, 120
Son of a rector and descended through his mother from the poet
John Donne. 'The Task' is thought to be his greatest work.

GEORGE CRABBE (1754–1832) 27, 33
Lived in Aldeburgh, Suffolk. Good narrative poet.

C. H. O. DANIEL (1845–1919) 100
Oxford clergyman, poet and publisher.

W. H. DAVIES (1871–1940) 63
British poet who travelled in the USA and wrote 'The
Autobiography of a Super-tramp' in 1908. Discovered by
George Bernard Shaw.

C. L. GRAVES 98
Published in *Punch* during the First World War.

JULIAN GRENFELL (1888–1915) 55
Eldest son of Lord Desborough. Soldier poet, killed in action and awarded the DSO. 'Into Battle' is thought to be his finest poem.

LORD GRENVILLE (1759–1834) 52
English statesman, died at the family estate in Dropmore.

LOUISE IMOGEN GUINEY (1861–1920) 124
American essayist and poet.

THOM GUNN (b. 1929) 18, 171
Read English at Cambridge and was published while still an undergraduate. Teaches at the University of California and lives in San Francisco.

SUSAN HAMLYN 117
Teacher of English language and literature in London, has published widely in poetry magazines and anthologies as well as her own collections.

THOMAS HARDY (1840–1928) 62, 85
From a rather poor family, he was a prolific novelist and poet and wrote much about his native West Country.

SIR JOHN HARINGTON (1561–1612) 23
English courtier and writer, godson of Queen Elizabeth.

FRANCIS BRET HARTE (1836–1902) 29
American author and statesman, lived in England in later life.

JO HASLAM (b. 1949) 31
Contemporary writer and freelance artist, who has had two collections of poems published; she still misses her dog.

SEAMUS HEANEY (b. 1939) 134
Irish poet awarded the Nobel Prize for Literature in 1995, produced an award-winning translation of 'Beowulf'.

ROBERT HERRICK (1591–1674) 43
English poet, Cambridge graduate and royalist.

T. HODGKINSON 119
Published in *Punch*.

HOMER (ninth century BC) 32
Greek epic poet. His most famous translator into English was George Chapman, who published both the *Iliad* and the *Odyssey* in 1616. Several other poets followed with translations through the centuries, those of Alexander Pope being another significant body of work.

P. HORRIDGE 17
Veterinary surgeon. Published 1998.

TED HUGHES (1930–99) 168
English poet, born in Yorkshire, educated at Pembroke College, Cambridge. Poet Laureate.

COLIN HURRY 97
Wrote 'The Oracle Dog and the Sages,' 1954.

ROBIN IVY (b. 1919) 41
Born in Bedford, a keen naturalist and animal lover who has published several poems. Member of a Cambridge poetry group.

FRANCIS JAMMES (1869–1938) 127
French writer, whose poems show a deep love of the countryside.

GLYN JONES (b. 1905) 92
Welsh poet and story-teller.

JENNY JOSEPH (b. 1932) 186
British poet.

RUDYARD KIPLING (1865–1936) 1, 67, 132, 201
Born in Bombay. His father was the curator of the Lahore Museum with interests in several arts. He was educated in England at the United Services' College in Devonshire, but returned to India in 1882 to become a journalist. He wrote many novels, poems and children's stories, mainly about India.

HENRY LAWSON (1867–1922) 36, 111, 143
Australian writer of stories and verse about the Australian scene.

R.C. LEHMANN (1856–1929) 105, 130
Liberal MP and journalist on *Punch*, father of the actress Beatrix and the novelist Rosamund.

WINIFRED M. LETTS 128
Writer of prose, verse and plays in the 1930s, and books for children. Educated and lived in Dublin.

GWYNETH LEWIS 95
Contemporary poet.

E. V. LUCAS (1868–1938) 45
English essayist and biographer, contributor to *Punch*.

NORMAN MacCAIG (b. 1910) 61, 192
Scottish poet, educated at Edinburgh University.

SORLEY MacLEAN (b. 1911) 30
Born on the Scottish island of Raasay, he had spent most of his life working as a school teacher and headmaster. He was wounded at El Alamein during the Second World War.

LOUIS MacNEICE (1907–63) 177
Born in Belfast. Joined the BBC in 1941 and wrote many radio scripts, as well as being an established poet.

SIR HENRY NEWBOLT (1862–1938) 190
Barrister, poet and dramatist, best-known for his sea songs.

LESLIE NORRIS 60
Contemporary poet.

WILL H. OGILVIE (1869–1963) 38, 148, 152
Born in Kelso, Scotland. From 1889 to 1901 he worked in
Australia as a drover, horse breaker and bush worker, writing
poems and ballads about his experiences. He then settled back
in Scotland as a farmer, writer and countryman, though he
spent two years lecturing in the USA.

FIONA OWEN 138
Born in Switzerland, grew up in Arabia and has settled in
Wales. She teaches creative writing and runs Anglesey Writers
Group and Ucheldre Literary Society.

GARY PAULSEN (b. 1939) 194
American author of children's books.

L. R. PHELPS 99
Oxford poet at the end of the nineteeth century.

PINDAR (*c.* 552–*c.* 404 BC) 189
The chief lyric poet of Greece.

RUTH PITTER (b. 1897) 48
English poet, encouraged by Hilaire Belloc. Winner of the
Hawthornden Prize in 1936.

ALEXANDER POPE (1688–1744) 42, 104, 122
One of the greatest English poets, well-known for his metrical
skills. The child of elderly parents, he was not physically robust.
He translated many classical works, including the *Iliad* in about
1717.

JACK PRELUTSKY 75
Contemporary author of poems for children.

RICHARD WILBUR (b. 1921) 81
American award-winning poet, Poet Laureate of the USA,
1987–8.

WILLIAM WORDSWORTH (1770–1850) 15, 83, 142
One of the great Romantic poets, he was born in Cumberland
and spent most of his life there, although he also travelled wide-
ly in Europe. He became Poet Laureate in 1843.

RALPH WOTHERSPOON 72
British poet.

JAMES WRIGHT (1927–80) 82
American poet.

INDEX OF FIRST
LINES OF POEMS
OR EXTRACTS

References are to poem numbers.

Who's this – alone with stone and sky? 3
With eye upraised, his master's looks to scan 33

Yellow wheels and red wheels, wheels that squeak and roar
     35
Your little Dog that bark'd as I came by 23
You see this dog. It was but yesterday 19
You that pass me, do not sneer 84
You who wander hither 54

PUBLISHER'S
ACKNOWLEDGEMENTS

The publishers wish to acknowledge the sources and permissions sought for poems and extracts reproduced in this collection, and to apologise to any copyright holders who could not be traced or who have been inadvertently overlooked.

'Crackers' and 'Walking the dogs' by Judith Adams, by permission of the author.
'Our puppy' by Pauline Anderson, by permission of the author.
'Liz' by Peter Arthur, by permission of the author.
'Stay, Go and Fetch' by Les Barker, by permission of the author and Mrs Ackroyd Records.
'Liquorice' by William Beaumont, from *A kennel of dogs*.
'Teddy' by the Rt Hon David Blunkett MP, by permission of the author.
'A child's dream' by Francis Cornford, Trustees of Mrs F.C. Cornford.
'Tom's little dog' by Walter de la Mare, Literary Trustees of Walter de la Mare, and The Society of Authors as their literary representative.
'Daughter' by Hester Dunlop, by permission of the author.
'Pekes and Pollicles' by T.S. Eliot, from *Old Possum's Book of Practical Cats*, by permission of Faber & Faber Ltd.
'A dog's eye view' by Roger Elkin, by permission of the author.
'For a lurcher' by Rob Evans, by permission of the author.
'Bliss', 'Inside' and 'Outside' by Eleanor Farjeon, David Higham Associates.

'To my dog' and 'In memory of my dog' by Cecil Floersheim, from *Collected Poems* (Messrs Combridges, Hove, 1936).
'Blue' by Roger Garfitt, by permission of the author.
'Landscape: dog looking at a bird' by Philip Gell, by permission of the author.
'Dogs' by Harry Ghisi, by permission of Roger Elkin.
'Wild thing' by Ben Gimson, by permission of the author.
'Sorrel' by Nathaniel Gimson, by permission of the author.
'Her pet' and 'Yoko' by Thom Gunn, from *Selected Poems*, by permission of Faber & Faber Ltd.
'Attila takes a hand' by Susan Hamlyn, by permission of the author.
'The dog's heart' by Jo Haslam, by permission of the author.
'A dog was crying tonight in Wicklow also' by Seamus Heaney, from *The Spirit Level*, by permission of Faber & Faber Ltd.
'The partners' by P. Horridge, from *In Newer Veins* (Primrose Hill Press, 1998).
'Roger the dog' by Ted Hughes, from *What is the Truth*, by permission of Faber & Faber Ltd.
'Sam' by Colin Hurry, from *The Oracle Dog and the Sages* (1954).
'Dogs' by Robin Ivy, by permission of the author.
'Remembering Siani' by Glyn Jones, by permission of Combrógos.
'Dog body and cat mind' by Jenny Joseph, Virago Press.
'Good dog!' by Gwyneth Lewis, by permission of the author and Bloodaxe.
'Praise of a collie' and 'Angus's dog' by Norman MacCaig, from *Collected Poems 1990* (Chatto & Windus).
'Dogs and wolves' by Sorley MacLean, from *Dàin do Eimhir* (1943).
'PC Plod and the Dale Street dog strangler' by Roger McGough, by permission of Peters, Fraser and Dunlop.
'The Victor dog' and 'My father's Irish Setters' by James Merrill, Alfred Knopf.
'The dog lovers' and 'My boyhood dog' by Spike Milligan, by permission of Spike Milligan Productions Ltd.
'Deer Hound' by Leslie Norris, by permission of Combrógos.

'The little dog from nowhere' by Derek Neville, from *The Little Dog from Nowhere* (Norwich, Gildengate Press, 1973).

'Dandie Dinmonts', 'The white hound' and 'Alone with hounds' by Will H. Ogilvie, published by Constable by permission of George T.A. Ogilvie.

'The dog shoot' by Fiona Owen, by permission of the author.

'Digdog' by Ruth Pitter, from *Poems 1926-66* (Barrie & Rockliff, London).

'Hello! How are you? I am fine!' by Jack Prelutsky, by permission of Egmont Children's Books.

'The sea' by James Reeves, by permission of Egmont Children's Books.

'Dim dog' and 'Collie romance' by Alan Ross, from *Island of the Children* (Orchard Books).

Extract from 'The land' by V. Sackville-West, *The Land* © 1927 by Vita-Sackville-West, reproduced by permission of Curtis Brown London on behalf of the Estate of Vita Sackville-West.

'Man and dog' by Siegfried Sassoon, George Sassoon.

'Muse' by Jo Shapcott, from *Phrase Book* (Oxford University Press).

'Sonnet' by Ann Smith, by permission of the author.

'A dog's death' and 'To a bull-dog' by Sir John Squire, from *Poems in One Volume* (William Heinemann Ltd).

'The dog in the manger' by Joe Walker from *That Dog of Mine*, and 'Waiting up for master' and 'Buried treasure' from *My Dog and Yours* (Ward Lock).